Python3.3.4 Tkinter/Ttk Widgets and Sqlite3
For Windows and Debian-Linux Includes Source Code
Python language runs on most operating systems

First Edition

Herb Norbom

Author of:
Raspberry Pi GPS using Python For Windows and Debian-Linux
Raspberry Pi Camera Controls For Windows and Debian-Linux using Python 3.2
Raspberry Pi Camera Controls For Windows and Debian-Linux using Python 2.7
Raspberry Pi Robot with Camera and Sound
Raspberry Pi Robot with Camera and Sound using Python 3.2.3
Robot Wireless Control Made Simple with Python and C
Python Version 2.6 Introduction using IDLE
Python Version 2.7 Introduction using IDLE
Python Version 3.2 Introduction using IDLE and PythonWin
Bootloader Source Code for ATMega168 using STK500 For Microsoft Windows
Bootloader Source Code for ATMega168 using STK500 For Debian-Linux
Bootloader Source Code for ATMega328P using STK500 For Microsoft Windows
Bootloader Source Code for ATMega328P using STK500 For Debian-Linux
Books Available on Amazon and CreateSpace

Where we are aware of a trademark that name has been printed with a Capital Letter.

Great care has been taken to provide accurate information, by both the author and the publisher, no expressed or implied warranty of any kind is given. No liability is assumed for any damages in connection with any information provided.

Table of Contents

FOREWARD

Congratulations on selecting Python, you have made a great choice. Python is a dynamic and relatively easy to use interpretive programming language. Python is available for most computer operating systems, and your Python programs can be relatively easily ported between the various operating systems. Python has a very good standard GUI in Tkinter/Ttk. The biggest shortfall could be considered to be the documentation of the GUI for the beginner to intermediate programmer. There is a wealth of information on the web and in the Python documentation. The problem I have found is that examples are not as clear as they could be and you must search a number of sites to find relevant information. This book is aimed at filling that gap for the programmer that wants to enhance their code with GUI's and data storage using Sqlite3. Sqlite3 is also included in the standard Python system.

PREFACE

This book grew out of my desire to have a desktop reference that gave me quick look up of GUI functions and Sqlite3 commands. Short examples are provided using Python 3.3.4. The development shown has been done on a Windows XP system, however all the examples are tested on Debian Linux using the Raspberry Pi Wheezy operating system. (The Appendix has a summary of the hardware and operating systems used). I am going to keep the examples as simple as possible. With a basic understanding of the widgets their use in complex programs will be much easier. We are going to focus on Ttk which at this point consists of seventeen widgets, most of which existed in Tkinter. We will focus on Ttk because it has the enhanced features and functions without the loss, I think, of any Tkinter features. We will cover the basic Tkinter widgets to provide continuity. With Ttk there are six new widgets that greatly enhance the overall appeal of Ttk. We are also going to cover Python's Sqlite3 in particular how to display data using the Ttk Treeview. We will cover the basics of setting up the database, including: adding, deleting, and modifying data and linking data.

 I am going to provide complete working examples. I am not going to go into the same depth in explaining the code as I did in my first book   'Robot Wireless Control Made Simple with Python and C', where I covered queuing, threading, communication, etc. If you are just starting with Python consider my book 'Python Version 3.2 Introduction using IDLE and PythonWin'. If you are interested you can search Amazon using my name for a complete list of books.

Python Start

Check your Python version and set up a work directory. I called my directory 'RyMax'. I set mine up in the default directory where the command prompt opens. I will use the Programmer's NotePad as my editor. The Appendix has additional information. Have a look at the Python 3.3 Documentation; it was probably installed with the software.

The following walks you through your first Python program using a Windows PC. The process for running from Debian-Linux is similar to the Windows process. See the Appendix for getting this working.

Python needs to be in your system path. For Windows you may need to add Python to your path. You can see what the system path is, from the command line type 'path'. If Python is not shown you need to add it. The simplest method is to create a batch file that you execute from the command line. You can also add to your environment, but I am not going to cover that.

I created the following bat file to set the path to python, you need to run this bat file each time you open the command prompt to setup the path. The path statement in the batch file appends the path to Python on a temporary base. When you close the command prompt the path is dropped by the system.

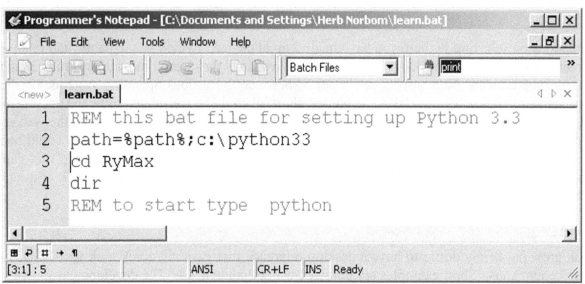

Text 1: BatFile

You may notice in the bat file and in the results exhibit that I included the path statement. In the following exhibit the results from starting the cmd prompt to executing the 'learn.bat' file to starting Python3.3 are shown.

Text 2: DOScmd

To exit the Python prompt you can enter "Crtl z" and press Return; will exit to your command prompt.

For Linux, see the Appendix, images are located in different directories, and I will show you the file I used to add Python to the path.

Let us make a very small Python program. I suggest you leave the command prompt open in our RyMax directory, as we will create and save our first program or script in that directory. In this program we are going to create a Window with our first button and the button will close the window when pressed. I will use my editor to create the program and run the program from the command prompt once I have saved it.

Tkinter Module

We will use the standard interface that is generally included with Python 3.3.x, the Tkinter/Ttk module. If you need to upgrade your version of Python or are missing a module I suggest you visit ActiveState or SourceForge Web sites.

If you have been looking at Tkinter/Ttk on the web you have probably seen that there are a number of ways to import or load the modules. I am going to use the method that is documented in the ActivePython3.3 Documentation. With this method the basic Tk widgets are automatically replaced with the Ttk widgets as appropriate. An advantage is that you do not need to specify ttk or tk widgets, you get ttk when available. The disadvantage is that you may not know when you are using tk vs ttk widgets. While automatic is not always better, there is a little less typing. A widget is a module, for example a button, label, etc. I am going to use the widget name, for example 'Button' and not specify it as Tkinter or Ttk.

As you get familiar with Tkinter/Ttk you will see that there are a large number of configuration options available for each widget. My mind would be worn out if I tried to show an example for each configuration option for each widget. Luckily for the most part the configuration options work pretty much the same for each widget, there of course different options for some widgets.

Button

We are going to program a simple GUI (Graphical User Interface). In the Programmer's Notepad open a new Python worksheet, enter the following and save as 'Tk1Button.py'. The 'py' extension is needed.

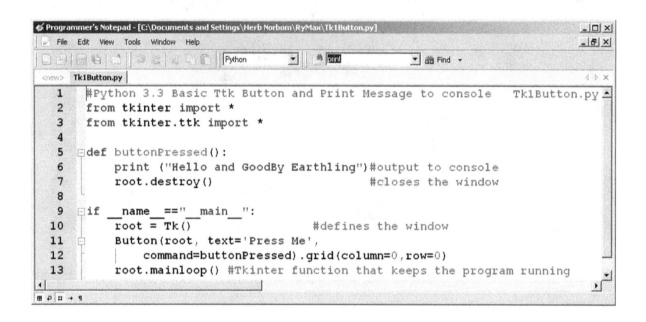

Text 3: simpleButton

Think of the actions required to produce this user control and output. I hope that you see the power of Python and Tkinter/Ttk. relative to other programming languages. The actual 'Button' line has a structure to it. The widget name is Button; we want the button to appear in the 'root' window. The text of the button will be 'Press Me'. If the button is pressed the button depresses and the program runs or calls the procedure or function 'buttonPressed'. Grid is a whole concept by itself. For now, just know we need it there or the button will not display. When you press the button, click on it with the mouse and you will see it depress, then bounce back. The program ran the procedure we specified.

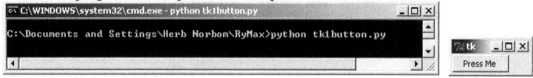

Text 4: Simple Button Result

When you press the button the window closes and the message is printed to the console.

Window Title, Size, Position, Style and Theme

We are going to take our Tk1Button.py program and add a window title, size it a bit and place it on the screen. First let us change the size. Add the following line to your program. I like to put the line in below the root.title line. root.geometry ("500x100+200+10"):

- 500 is the width of the window or the x axis
- 100 is the height of the window or the y axis
- 200 is the position on your display screen, from the top left hand corner, going along the x axis. The top left corner of the display screen is position (0,0)
- 10 is the position on your display screen down from the top, along the y axis.

We will also introduce the 'Ttk themed widgets' which we will use to customize the look of our widgets. We first have to define our 'Style' class. This is done by setting 'Style()' equal to a class name, so that we can work with or configure it. The next step is to define a 'theme"; I like the 'classic' theme. Your choices include: 'winnative', 'clam', 'alt', 'default', and 'classic'. The next step is to configure 'style' which I called 'BT' in the program example. The first item of the configuration is the 'STYLE NAME' you want to use. In the example I used 'exit.TButton'. I could have just used 'TButton'. The style option provides a great way to standardize your widgets. I am saving my program as Tk2winSize.py. You will note in the code that I have commented out a number of lines. I included them so you could play with different color and some of the methods of defining the color. The 'font' example is provided to show size and features. We are not going to use all the Style Names at the moment but a complete list for the various widgets follows.

Style Name

WIDGET	STYLE NAME
Button	TButton
Checkbutton	TCheckbutton
Combobox	TCombobox
Entry	TEntry
Frame	TFrame
Label	TLabel
LabelFrame	TLabelFrame
Menubutton	TMenubutton
Notebook	TNotebook
PanedWindow	TPanedwindow
Progressbar	Horizontal.TProgressbar or Vertical.TProgressbar
Radiobutton	TRadiobutton
Scale	Horizontal.TScale or Vertical.TScale
Scrollbar	Horizontal.TScrollbar or Vertical.TScrollbar
Separator	TSeparator

Sizegrip	TSizegrip
Treeview	Treeview

Of course each of the Styles/Themes have options that can vary.

```
Programmer's Notepad - [C:\Documents and Settings\Herb Norbom\RyMax\Tk2winSize.py *]
File  Edit  View  Tools  Window  Help
                                      Python        print          Find

<new>  Tk2winSize.py *

 1   #Python 3.3 Window title, size and placement start using style    Tk2winSize.py
 2   from tkinter import *
 3   from tkinter.ttk import *
 4   def buttonPressed():
 5       print ("You will win")                    #output to console
 6       root.destroy()                            #closes the window
 7   def button():
 8       BT=Style()  #for all buttons in program
 9       # could use 'winnative','clam','alt','default','classic','xpnative'
10       BT.theme_use('alt') #you need to define the theme prior to using configure
11       BT.configure('exit.TButton',
12   #         foreground='navy',                        # standard system colors
13   #         foreground='#%02x%02x%02x' %(0,0,255),    # navy  using decimal
14   #         foreground='#0000ff',                     # navy using hex
15             foreground='#ffffff',                     # white 255 255 255
16             background='#%02x%02x%02x' %(00,00,00),   #black
17             font ='helvetica 34 bold italic',
18             relief='groove'),    #options are raised,sunken,flat,ridge,solid,groove
19       Button1=Button(root,
20           text='use exit.TButton style',
21           command=buttonPressed,
22           style='exit.TButton')
23       Button1.grid(column=0,row=0)
24   if __name__=="__main__":
25       root = Tk()                    #defines the window
26       root.title("RyMax Window on the world")
27       root.geometry("500x100+200+10")#width, height, x location, y location
28       button()
29       root.mainloop() # Tkinter function that keeps the program running
```

Text 5: WindowSizeStyle

Notice the changes when the mouse hovers over the window. We will spend more time on the Style as this concept applies to many of the Tkinter/Ttk widgets. One other item I want to mention, notice how I moved the grid to line 23. Not sure why but having it set up this way helps to ensure your commands work.

Text 6: WindowSizeStyleResults

Toplevel Window

In our next example we will use a button to open a second window. The second window will have a button to close itself. Notice the different setting for the buttons, but only one theme for all the buttons.

```python
1   #Python 3.3 second window expand style, button close second window          Tk3secWin.py
2   from tkinter import *
3   from tkinter.ttk import *
4   def buttonPressed():
5       print ("You have done well")     #output to console
6       TOP=Toplevel()
7       TOP.title("RyMax SECOND Window")
8       TOP.geometry("300x200+200+100") #width, height, x location, y location
9       Button(TOP, text='Press to close Second Window',command=TOP.destroy,
10          style='exit.TButton').grid(column=0,row=0)
11  def button2Pressed(): print ("Is it you?")      #output to console
12  def button3Pressed(): print ("Are you him?")    #output to console
13  def button():
14      BT=Style()                      #for all buttons in program
15      BT.theme_use('classic')#'winnative','clam','alt','default','classic','xpnative'
16      BT.configure('TButton',foreground='blue',background='white')     # default settings
17      BT.configure('exit.TButton',foreground='yellow',background='red')# exit settings
18      Button(root, text='use exit.TButton settings',command=buttonPressed,
19          style='exit.TButton').grid(column=0,row=0)
20      BT.configure('C.TButton',foreground='pink',background='gray')
21      Button(root, text='use C.TButton settings',command=button2Pressed,
22          style='C.TButton').grid(column=1,row=0)
23      Button(root, text='use default settings',command=button3Pressed).grid(column=2,row=0)
24  if __name__=="__main__":
25      root = Tk()                      #defines the window
26      root.title("RyMax Window on the world")
27      root.geometry("500x100+200+10")#width, height, x location, y location
28      button()
29      root.mainloop() # Tkinter function that keeps the program running
```

Text 7: secondWindow

You can see the theme changed. When you press the button on the second window it will close just that window.

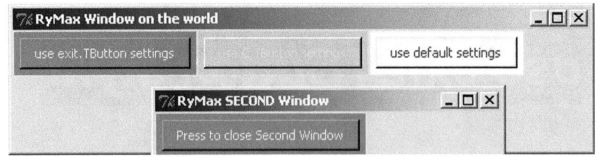

Text 8: secondWindowResults

Button with Image

Add a picture to your widget. In the following we add a 'gif' image from the Python33\tcl\tk8.5\demos\images directory. Some other interesting gif's are commented out, try as you like.

```
#Python 3.3 add image to button                    Tk4image.py
from tkinter import *
from tkinter.ttk import *
def buttonPressed():
    print ("You will win")              #output to console
    root.destroy()                      #closes the window
def button():
    BT=Style()
    BT.theme_use('clam')
    BT.configure('exit.TButton',
        foreground='#ffffff',  background='#%02d%02d%02d' %(128,192,200),
        relief='raised') #options 'raised,sunken,flat,ridge,solid,groove'
    Button1=Button(root,
        text='use exit.TButton style',
        command=buttonPressed,
        image=myImage,
        style='exit.TButton')
    Button1.grid(column=0,row=0)
if __name__=="__main__":
    root = Tk()
    root.title("RyMax Window on the world")
    root.geometry("500x300+200+10")#width, height, x location, y location
#   myImage=PhotoImage(file='c:/python33/tcl/tk8.5/images/logo64.gif')
#   myImage=PhotoImage(file='c:/python33/lib/idlelib/icons/python.gif')
    myImage=PhotoImage(file='c:/python33/tcl/tk8.5/demos/images/earth.gif')
#   myImage=PhotoImage(file='c:/python33/tcl/tk8.5/demos/images/earthris.gif')
    button()
    root.mainloop()
```

Text 9: ButtonImage

Notice how the button expanded automatically.

Text 10: Button Image Result

Changing Button Text

A nice feature is to be able to change the text displaying on the button when it is pressed. I used the 'classic' theme because some of the other themes did not show the highlight color area very clearly.

```python
#Python 3.3.4          textvariable for button          Tk5textVar.py
from tkinter import *
from tkinter.ttk import *
def Pressed():
    if myText.get()=='NO':
        myText.set('YES')
    else:
        myText.set('NO')

def button():
    BT=Style()
    BT.theme_use('classic')
    BT.configure('exit.TButton',foreground='gold',  background='black',
        relief='raised', highlightcolor='green')
    Button1=Button(root,
        textvariable=myText, command=Pressed, style='exit.TButton')
    Button1.grid(column=0,row=0)

if __name__=="__main__":
    root = Tk()
    root.title("RyMax Window on the world")
    root.geometry("170x75+200+10")#width, height, x location, y location
    myText=StringVar()
    myText.set('YES')
    button()
    root.mainloop()
```

Text 11: ButtonVariableText

Map for Theme

The theme concept with the map provides a very strong method of quickly defining unique qualities to your entire program without a great deal of repetitive coding. In the following click on the buttons and note the interactive changes in the display window.

```python
#Python 3.3.4    the map feature                    Tk6.py
from tkinter import *
from tkinter.ttk import *
def Pressed():
    if myText.get()=='NO':
        myText.set('YES')
    else:
        myText.set('NO')
def Pressed2():
    if myText2.get()=='NO':
        myText2.set('YES')
    else:
        myText2.set('NO')
def button():
    BT=Style()   #for all buttons in program
    BT.theme_use('classic')
    BT.configure('exit.TButton',
        background='blue',
        foreground='white',
        highlightthickness='5',
        font =('helvetica 34 bold italic'))
```

Text 12: MapFeature1

File   Edit   View   Tools   Window   Help

Python ▼   print ▼   Find ▼

<new> | Tk1.py | Tk2.py | Tk3.py | Tk4.py | TkS.py | **Tk6.py**

```
22        BT.map('exit.TButton',
23            foreground=[('disabled','yellow'),
24                         ('pressed','red'),
25                         ('active','blue')],
26            background=[('disabled','black'),
27                         ('pressed','cyan'),
28                         ('active','green')],
29            highlightcolor=[('focus','green'),
30                            ('!focus','red')],
31            relief=[('pressed', 'groove'),
32                    ('!pressed', 'raised')])
33        Button1=Button(root,
34            textvariable=myText,command=Pressed,style='exit.TButton')
35        Button1.grid(column=0,row=0)
36        Button2=Button(root,
37            textvariable=myText2,command=Pressed2,style='exit.TButton')
38        Button2.grid(column=1,row=0)
39  if __name__=="__main__":
40        root = Tk()
41        root.title("RyMax Window on the world")
42        root.geometry("500x100+200+10")#width, height, x location, y location
43        myText=StringVar()
44        myText.set('YES')
45        myText2=StringVar()
46        myText2.set('NO')
47        button()
48        root.mainloop() # Tkinter function that keeps the program running
```

Text 13: MapFeature2

Text 14: MapFeature

Variable Image for your Button

You may find that adding images to your buttons brings a very sophisticated look to your programs. To add some more visual candy lets change the image when the button is pressed. We are going to continue working with gif's and note where we are switching them it is best if they are the same size. In the following code I have commented out the third image. Play with an image of a different size by removing the comment and placing the '#' on the previous line.

```
  1   #Python 3.3.4    the map feature with variable image          Tk7varImage.py
  2   from tkinter import *
  3   from tkinter.ttk import *
  4   def Pressed():
  5       pass              #lets us define a function that does nothing
  6   def setup_widgets():
  7       BT=Style(root)   #for all buttons in program
  8       BT.theme_use('classic')
  9       BT.configure('exit.TButton',
 10           background='blue',foreground='white',highlightthickness='5',
 11           font =('helvetica 34 bold italic'))
 12       BT.map('exit.TButton',
 13           foreground=[('disabled','yellow'),('pressed','red'),('active','blue')],
 14           background=[('disabled','black'),('pressed','cyan'),('active','green')],
 15           highlightcolor=[('focus','green'),('!focus','red')],
 16           image=(('!pressed',myImage),('pressed',myImage2)),
 17           relief=[('pressed', 'groove'),('!pressed', 'raised')])
 18       Button1=Button(root,
 19           command=Pressed,style='exit.TButton')
 20       Button1.grid(column=0,row=0)
 21   if __name__=="__main__":
 22       root = Tk()
 23       root.title("RyMax Window on the world")
 24       root.geometry("500x235+200+10")#width, height, x location, y location
 25       myImage=PhotoImage(file='c:/python33/tcl/tk8.5/demos/images/earth.gif')
 26       myImage2=PhotoImage(file='c:/python33/tcl/tk8.5/demos/images/earthris.gif')
 27   #   myImage2=PhotoImage(file='c:/python33/lib/idlelib/icons/python.gif')
 28       setup_widgets()
 29       root.mainloop()
```

Text 15: Map Variable Image

CheckButton with Map and Variable Text

This is a useful button for turning features on and off. When you link the CheckButton to other widgets or what actions to take in your program you can easily have the user control the program. In the following I expanded the map features and as you will see selected some color combinations that you will probably not want to use.

```
      #Python 3.3.4  Check Button with variable text and map      Tk8CheckButton.py
 1
 2    from tkinter import *
 3    from tkinter.ttk import *
 4   ⊟def getStatus():
 5        print (ckStatus.get())
 6        if ckStatus.get()=='ON':
 7            myText.set('I am On')
 8        else:
 9            myText.set('I am Off')
10   ⊟if __name__=="__main__":
11        root = Tk()
12        root.title("RyMax Window on the world")
13        root.geometry("500x100+200+10")#width, height, x location, y location
14        BT=Style(root)
15        BT.theme_use('classic')
16        BT.configure('exit.TButton' )
17        BT.map('exit.TButton',foreground=[('pressed','red'),('active','blue')],
18            background=[('!active','yellow'),('pressed','cyan'),('active','green')],
19            font =[('active',('Times','20','bold','underline')),('!active',('Sans 20'))],
20            highlightcolor=[('focus','green'),('!focus','red')],
21            highlightthickness=[('!active',10),('active', 5)],
22            relief=[('pressed', 'groove'),('!pressed','raised')])
23        ckStatus = StringVar()
24        myText = StringVar()
25        myText.set('I am On')
26        checkStatus = Checkbutton(root, style='exit.TButton',textvariable=myText,
27            variable=ckStatus, onvalue='ON', offvalue='OFF', command= getStatus)
28        checkStatus.grid(column=0,row=0)
29        root.mainloop()
```

Text 16: CheckButton

I have combined three of the possible results in the following exhibit.

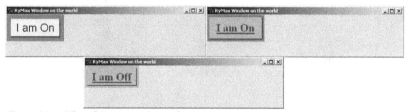

Text 17: CheckButton Results

Widget State checking and setting

As your programs become more complex you may want to check the 'state' of the widget, and/or set the 'state'. The 'states' are 'normal', 'active' and 'disabled'. I am sure you noticed we have been using the states to some degree with our 'map'. I went ahead and added a little more functionality to our program by setting up the 'class Buttons'. I also added a very simple 'init' function. The purpose of the 'class' and the 'init' are to add structure to our program and to greatly facilitate the moving of variables between functions. Two buttons are on the window, they share the same theme and map. Pressing the first button will disable that button. Pressing the second button will make the first button active; notice the color changes as well.

```python
1   #Python 3.3.4 Ttk Button set and check the widget state    Tk9ChangeButtonState.py
2   from tkinter import *
3   from tkinter.ttk import *
4
5   class Buttons:
6       def __init__(self):
7           self.setup_widgets()
8
9       def setup_widgets(self):
10          self.BT=Style(root)
11          self.BT.theme_use('classic')
12          self.BT.configure('exit.TButton')
13          self.BT.map('exit.TButton',
14              foreground=[('disabled','yellow'),('pressed','red'),('active','blue')],
15              background=[('disabled','magenta'),('pressed','cyan'),('active','green')],
16              highlightcolor=[('focus','green'),('!focus','red')],
17              relief=[('pressed', 'groove'),('!pressed', 'ridge')])
18          self.Button1=Button(root, text='Press to Disable Button1',command=self.Press1,
19              style='exit.TButton')
20          self.Button1.grid(column=0,row=0)
21          self.Button2=Button(root, text='Press to Enable Button1',command=self.Press2,
22          style='exit.TButton')
23          self.Button2.grid(column=1,row=0)
```

Text 18: Change Button State

```python
24
25      def Press1(self):
26          print (self.Button1.state())
27          self.Button1.config(state='disabled')
28
29      def Press2(self):
30          self.Button1.config(state='normal') #or use 'active' for our purpose
31          print (self.Button1.state())
32
33  if __name__=="__main__":
34      root = Tk()
35      root.title("RyMax Window on the world")
36      root.geometry("320x50+200+10")#width, height, x location, y location
37      Buttons()
38      root.mainloop()
39
```

Text 19: Change Button State2

I have combined several of the possible results in the following exhibit.

Text 20: WidgetStateCheckSetResults

Entry

We will in many cases want our users to input data to the program. This is made fairly easy with the 'Entry Widget'. There some rules you need to be aware of. What you input will be treated as a string by Python. Also this widget is just for a single line of data. There are a lot of areas to cover that are important to you in developing a user friendly and 'bulletproof' program. We need to make sure that our user is entering somewhat what we want. We need to tell the user what we want, so we introduce the 'Label'. (More on Label later.) We need to validate the data the user entered, so we introduce validation. This program has a general validation version that occurs when the user presses return; the next program will go into more detail. We also introduce 'error trapping' sometimes called 'try and catch'. I would call this type validation 'after the fact'.

We have been using 'map' so I am just including it with the 'Entry' widget. The following program asks you to enter an integer within a range. In our first test we try to convert our entry to an integer, even though we entered an integer it is being processed within the Entry widget as a string. In our second test we do a simple 'if statement' to check the range of the input. If we fail a test we use the 'messagebox' to let the user know what error was made. (More on messagebox later.)

One method to display a value in the 'Entry Widget' is to define a variable and then insert that value into the 'Enter Widget'. Later on we will introduce the database and show how to insert values from our data files into our displays.

We need to be able to instruct our program to take action when the user presses a key. This is done by binding a 'key' to the widget. You can have multiple 'keys' bound to the same widget. In this program we bind three keys to the widget.

```python
#Python 3.3.4 Ttk Entry with validation Entry map & error trapping  Tk10EntryValidation.py
from tkinter import *
from tkinter.ttk import *
import tkinter.messagebox
class Buttons:
    def __init__(self):
        self.myInput=9999
        Label(root,text='Enter an integer from 1 to 9999').grid(column=1,row=0, sticky='nsew')
        self.setup_widgets()
    def setup_widgets(self):
        self.input=Style(root)
        self.input.theme_use('classic')
        self.input.configure('input.TEntry')
        self.input.map('input.TEntry',
            foreground=[('disabled','yellow'),('pressed','red'),('active','blue')],
            background=[('disabled','magenta'),('pressed','cyan'),('active','green')],
            highlightcolor=[('focus','green'),('!focus','red')],
            relief=[('pressed', 'groove'),('!pressed', 'ridge')])
        self.Entry1=Entry(root, style='input.TEntry')
        self.Entry1.insert(0,self.myInput)
        self.Entry1.grid(column=0,row=0)
        self.Entry1.bind("<Return>", self.validate)
        self.Entry1.bind("<KP_Enter>", self.validate)
        self.Entry1.bind("<F1>", self.myhelp)
        self.Entry1.focus()
```

Text 21: EntryWidget

```python
    def validate(self, event):
        testInput=self.Entry1.get()
        print (testInput)
        try:
            test=int(testInput)
        except:
            tkinter.messagebox.showwarning("Not Integer","Enter an Integer")
            return
        if (test < 1 ) | (test > 9999):
            tkinter.messagebox.showwarning("Out of Range","Enter range 1 to 9999")
            return
    def myhelp(self, event):
            tkinter.messagebox.showinfo("My Help Screen","Simple help info")
if __name__=="__main__":
    root = Tk()
    root.title("RyMax Window on the world")
    root.geometry("320x50+200+10")#width, height, x location, y location
    Buttons()
    root.mainloop()
```

Text 22: EntryWidget cont

Some of the output possibilities are shown in the following.

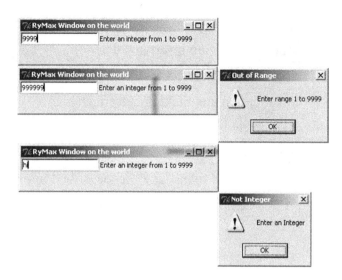

Text 23: EntryWidgetResults

More on Entry Validation

This is such an important concept that I wanted to provide more information. I have taken our previous example and dropped out a number of features to give an example that focuses on validation. We can build a callback into the 'Entry Widget'. This has several steps to it but once you get the concept it falls into place.

We can start with putting in something we are familiar with, a command to be executed. This validation can happen with each key stroke or when focus is lost or gained (move to another field). Your input is sent off to be validated, if your input passes validation it is then displayed in the 'Entry Widget'. You also define what is to be sent for validation, the keystroke or the entire value in the Entry Widget. In our Entry Widget we need to enter instructions on what to validate and where to do the validation.

When to validate is defined by the 'validate=' option. The choices are shown in the following table for when to do the validation.

none	Turns off validation
all	Validate all cases
focus	When focus is gained or lost on the Widget
focusin	When focus gained on the Widget
focusout	When the Widget looses focus
key	When a keystroke changes the data in the Widget

The next step is setting the statement to run when the validation action is triggered to occur. (Just like our command in other widgets.) This is the 'validationcommand='.

The next step is defining the statement that our 'validationcommand' will run. This gets a bit complicated as we need to use the 'register' to apply a wrapper to our function. The wrapper makes it easier to pass the substitution callback codes to our function where the actual validation occurs. The callback substitution codes are shown in the following table.

%d	Action code: 0 for attempted deletion, 1 for attempted insertion, -1 for focus change
%i	This marks an index for where to position insert and deletion
%P	If validation is successful this will be the new text, complete text as shown in the Entry
%s	The complete text prior to validation and making current change
%S	This is text being inserted or deleted
%v	Current value of the validation option
%V	The reason for the callback, change of focus, key, etc. described in previous table
%W	The name of the widget, if you do not name the widget Python assigns a number

Entry with Enhanced Validation

In the next program there are a number of items I would like to point out. First this is a program to show a number of features, in many cases you will find better ways to accomplish the same validation. I went to a somewhat lengthy test process to give you an idea that you can write just about any type of validation you want. It will help if we understand what is passed to the validation routine; when it is passed and what is returned. You can pass a single position string or the entire contents of the 'Entry'.

The first item to validate is an Integer. Sounds simple, but what if you have a negative value. And what if your user puts the negative sign on the end, or in the middle? As you look at the code you can see that I only allow the negative sign to precede the number. The value to test is sent as a string, so if we try to covert a letter or non-number to an integer we generate an error. Our error trapping handles that and then we test the first position of the text we are returning to see if we want to permit the negative sign. If the first character is the negative sign and we have input after that we need to test just that section of input, skipping the negative sign.

In Entry1the validatecommand includes the register. This shows that you can do the entire command in one line. As programs get more complex it may be nice to have it all together. Entry1 uses the 'key' option, so each key stroke is sent off for validation. We need to tell the program what to do when the user leaves the Entry field; this is where we bind in the action. This is different from the validation options show above. Valid bindings include the following examples.

<Return>	The Enter or Return key is pressed
<KP_Enter>	The Enter Key on the keypad is pressed
<F1>...<F12>	The function key F1 is pressed. Similar for other function keys
<FocusOut> <FocusIn>	The user moves off the field or on to the field
<Button-1>	User presses left mouse button,Button-2 for center, Button-3 for right
<B1-Motion>	User moved mouse while holding button down, similar case for B2 and B3 Motion
Special Keys	For the standard 102 keyboard, you can bind to just about all including: <Escape>, <Insert>, <Control_L>, <ALT_L>,<Pause>,<Prior>,<Next>,<Home>,<End>, <Num_Lock>,<Scroll_Lock>,arrow keys(<Left><Right><Up><Down>
<Key>	Any visible or printable key

There are methods to define special keys and modifiers, much more that I can handle at this point.

The following program tries to give you some different type of validation and methods of bindings. Entry2 uses the <Return> binding vs. <FocusOut> on the other lines, just to add a little variation. Needless to say in your program you will want to develop standards, makes for easier use and training.

All the Entry widgets use the 'name' option, which is not needed as Python assigns a number automatically if you do not give it a name. In Entry4 our output shows the name assigned to that Widget. The purpose of Entry4 is to show the data as it is processed through the validation. No actual validation is done.

Play with the program by trying various combinations of characters; try to break it. It is possible to confuse it.

```
Programmer's Notepad - [C:\Documents and Settings\Herb Norbom\RyMax\Tk11EntryValidation.py *]
File   Edit   View   Tools   Window   Help

[Python ▼]  [print ▼]  [Find ▼]

<new>   Tk11EntryValidation.py *

1    #Python 3.3.4 Ttk Entry, better validation and error trapping   Tk11EntryValidation.py
2    from tkinter import *
3    from tkinter.ttk import *
4    def vInteger(inText, outText):
5        testLength=len(outText)        #determine length of string outText
6        try:
7            inText = int(inText)
8        except:
9            if (testLength == 1 and outText[0]=='-'):        #test for negative number
10               return True
11           if testLength == 1:
12               return False
13           if testLength > 1:
14               try:
15                   test=int(outText[1:testLength])
16               except:
17                   return False
18               return True
19       return True
20   def vReal(inText,allText, outText):
21       lallText=len(allText)
22       if lallText==0:
23           try:
24               test=float(inText)
25               return True
26           except:
27               if ((inText=='-') | (inText=='.')):
28                   return True
29               return False
```

Text 24: Better Validation

File   Edit   View   Tools   Window   Help

Tk11EntryValidation.py *

```python
30          if lallText > 0:
31              try:
32                  test=float(inText)
33              except:
34                  if inText=='.':
35                      ctDecimal=outText.count('.')#count number of '.' in string outText
36                      if ctDecimal > 1:
37                          return False
38                      return True
39                  return False
40              return True
41  def vCharacter(inText, outText):
42      try:
43          inText = int(inText)
44          return False
45      except:
46          try:
47              inText = str.isalpha(inText)
48          except:
49              return False
50      return True
51  def vAll(d,i,P,s,S,v,V,W):
52      print ('Action Code d',d)
53      print ('insert/delete text i ',i)
54      print ('New Text Value P ',P)
55      print ('text before change s ',s)
56      print ('Text inserted/deleted S ',S)
57      print ('current value of validation v ',v)
58      print ('reason for callback V ',V)
```

Text 25: Better Validation2

```
59          print ('Widget Name W ',W)
60          print () #put a blank line in
61          return True
62   class Buttons:
63       def __init__(self):
64           self.cmd2 =root.register(vReal),"%S","%s","%P"
65           self.cmd3 =root.register(vCharacter),"%S","%P"
66           self.cmd4 =root.register(vAll),"%d","%i","%P","%s","%S","%v","%V","%W"
67           self.setup_widgets()
68       def setup_widgets(self):
69           Label (root,
70               text='Enter Integer(...,-10,0,1,2,55,...)').grid(column=1,row=0,sticky='nsew')
71           self.Entry1=Entry(root,name="entry1",validate='key',
72               validatecommand=(root.register(vInteger),"%S","%P"))
73           self.Entry1.grid(column=0,row=0)
74           self.Entry1.bind("<FocusOut>", self.finished)
75           self.Entry1.focus()
76           Label (root,
77               text='Enter real number(-10.0,-5,0,1,10.23)').grid(column=1,row=1,sticky='nsew')
78           self.Entry2=Entry(root,name="entry2",validate='key',validatecommand=self.cmd2)
79           self.Entry2.grid(column=0,row=1)
80           self.Entry2.bind("<Return>", self.finished2)
81           self.Entry2.focus()
82           Label (root,text='Enter Any non-number Character').grid(column=1,row=2,sticky='nsew')
83           self.Entry3=Entry(root,name="entry3",validate='key',validatecommand=self.cmd3)
84           self.Entry3.grid(column=0,row=2)
85           self.Entry3.bind("<FocusOut>", self.finished3)
86           self.Entry3.focus()
87           Label (root,text='Enter anything, ALL valid').grid(column=1,row=3,sticky='nsew')
```

Text 26: Better Validation3

File   Edit   View   Tools   Window   Help

<new>   Tk11EntryValidation.py *

```
 88            self.Entry4=Entry(root,name="entry4",validate='all',validatecommand=self.cmd4)
 89            self.Entry4.grid(column=0,row=3)
 90            self.Entry4.bind("<FocusOut>", self.finished4)
 91            self.Entry4.focus()
 92        def finished(self,event):
 93            if self.Entry1.get() != '':
 94                print ('Integer: ',self.Entry1.get())
 95                self.Entry2.focus()
 96        def finished2(self,event):
 97            if self.Entry2.get() != '':
 98                print ('Real: ',self.Entry2.get())
 99                self.Entry3.focus()
100        def finished3(self,event):
101            if self.Entry3.get() != '':
102                print ('Character: ',self.Entry3.get())
103                self.Entry4.focus()
104        def finished4(self,event):
105            if self.Entry4.get() != '':
106                print ('Any character or numeric:',self.Entry4.get())
107                self.Entry1.focus()
108 if __name__=="__main__":
109     root = Tk()
110     root.title("RyMax Window on the world")
111     root.geometry("400x150+200+10")#width, height, x location, y location
112     Buttons()
113     root.mainloop()
```

Text 27: Better Validation 4

Some results, just to give you an idea, I also included the command prompt screen to give a flavor to that output.

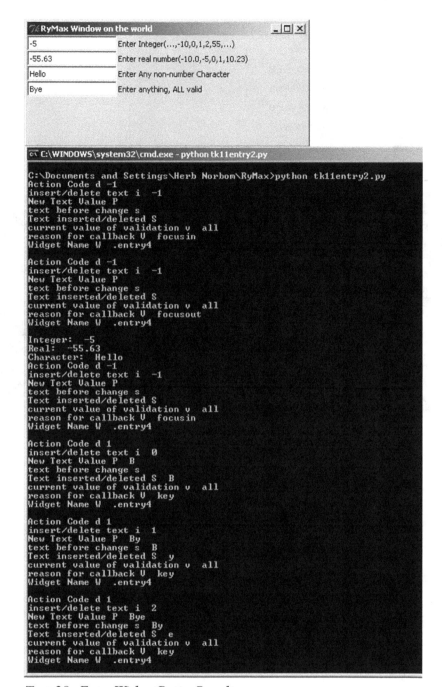

Text 28: EntryWidgetBetterResult

Event Binding

For your programs you will find that binding an event to a widget is a really nice feature. Not to mention it is really critical for you to control the user. In the following program I have given various binding examples. There are many more options than I can show, but I hope you get the idea and experiment. As you play with the program notice the console where the various results are printed. You can use the 'Tab' and 'Shift Tab' keys or the mouse to move between the Entry Widgets. To take the action and see results you need to do the action described in the Label.

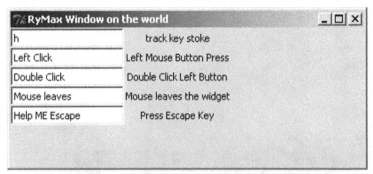

Text 29: EventBinding

Python   print   Find

<new>   Tk12EventBinding.py

```python
1    #Python 3.3.4 Ttk Entry with Event Biding Examples     Tk12EventBinding.py
2    from tkinter import *
3    from tkinter.ttk import *
4    class Buttons:
5        def __init__(self):
6            self.setup_widgets()
7        def setup_widgets(self):
8            Label(root, text='track key stoke').grid(column=1,row=0)
9            self.Entry1=Entry(root)
10           self.Entry1.grid(column=0,row=0)
11           self.Entry1.bind("<Key>", self.finished)
12           self.Entry1.focus()
13           Label(root, text='Left Mouse Button Press').grid(column=1,row=1)
14           self.Entry2=Entry(root)
15           self.Entry2.grid(column=0,row=1)
16           self.Entry2.bind("<Button-1>", self.finished2)
17           self.Entry2.focus()
18           Label(root,text='Double Click Left Button').grid(column=1,row=2)
19           self.Entry3=Entry(root)
20           self.Entry3.grid(column=0,row=2)
21           self.Entry3.bind("<Double-Button-1>", self.finished3)
22           self.Entry3.focus()
23           Label(root,text='Mouse leaves the widget').grid(column=1,row=3)
24           self.Entry4=Entry(root)
25           self.Entry4.grid(column=0,row=3)
26           self.Entry4.bind("<Leave>", self.finished4)
27           self.Entry4.focus()
```

Text 30: EventBindingProgram

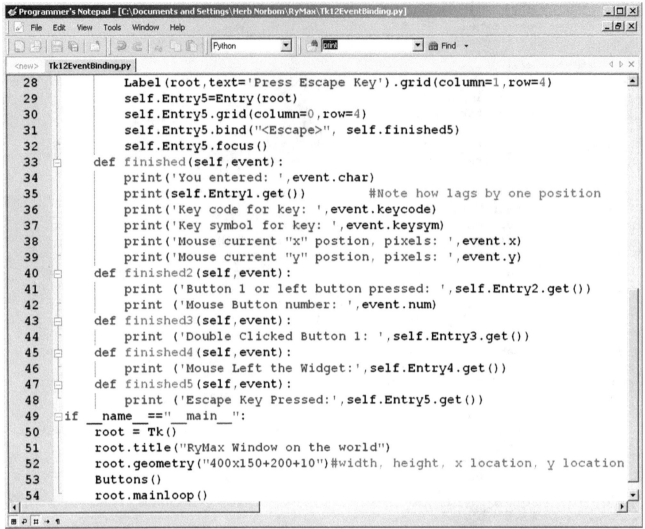

```
28          Label(root,text='Press Escape Key').grid(column=1,row=4)
29          self.Entry5=Entry(root)
30          self.Entry5.grid(column=0,row=4)
31          self.Entry5.bind("<Escape>", self.finished5)
32          self.Entry5.focus()
33      def finished(self,event):
34          print('You entered: ',event.char)
35          print(self.Entry1.get())          #Note how lags by one position
36          print('Key code for key: ',event.keycode)
37          print('Key symbol for key: ',event.keysym)
38          print('Mouse current "x" postion, pixels: ',event.x)
39          print('Mouse current "y" postion, pixels: ',event.y)
40      def finished2(self,event):
41          print ('Button 1 or left button pressed: ',self.Entry2.get())
42          print ('Mouse Button number: ',event.num)
43      def finished3(self,event):
44          print ('Double Clicked Button 1: ',self.Entry3.get())
45      def finished4(self,event):
46          print ('Mouse Left the Widget:',self.Entry4.get())
47      def finished5(self,event):
48          print ('Escape Key Pressed:',self.Entry5.get())
49  if __name__=="__main__":
50      root = Tk()
51      root.title("RyMax Window on the world")
52      root.geometry("400x150+200+10")#width, height, x location, y location
53      Buttons()
54      root.mainloop()
```

Text 31: EventBindingProgram2

Label with bitmap image

This is an import widget to understand because it is very useful in providing instructions and results to your user. We have been using the Label, but now we will go into some depth. As we have seen the Label can contain text or image or bitmap. The Button Widget has many examples for controlling fonts, background and etc using 'style' and 'map'. As these features are very similar our program we will use these but not go into depth on them.

Standard Python can handle gif and xbm (bitmap images) quite easily, example included in our program. The results are shown first to hopefully entice you. There are other modules available to you for handling other types of images, but you will need to download and install them. I am just trying to stay plain vanilla.

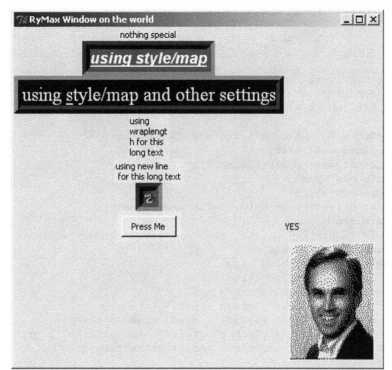

Text 32: LabelResults

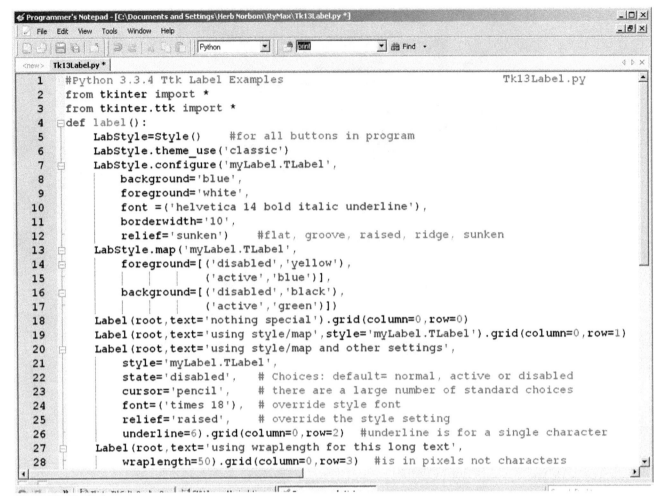

```python
#Python 3.3.4 Ttk Label Examples                          Tk13Label.py
from tkinter import *
from tkinter.ttk import *
def label():
    LabStyle=Style()       #for all buttons in program
    LabStyle.theme_use('classic')
    LabStyle.configure('myLabel.TLabel',
        background='blue',
        foreground='white',
        font =('helvetica 14 bold italic underline'),
        borderwidth='10',
        relief='sunken')       #flat, groove, raised, ridge, sunken
    LabStyle.map('myLabel.TLabel',
        foreground=[('disabled','yellow'),
                    ('active','blue')],
        background=[('disabled','black'),
                    ('active','green')])
    Label(root,text='nothing special').grid(column=0,row=0)
    Label(root,text='using style/map',style='myLabel.TLabel').grid(column=0,row=1)
    Label(root,text='using style/map and other settings',
        style='myLabel.TLabel',
        state='disabled',    # Choices: default= normal, active or disabled
        cursor='pencil',     # there are a large number of standard choices
        font=('times 18'),   # override style font
        relief='raised',     # override the style setting
        underline=6).grid(column=0,row=2)  #underline is for a single character
    Label(root,text='using wraplength for this long text',
        wraplength=50).grid(column=0,row=3)  #is in pixels not characters
```

Text 33: Label

```
29        Label(root,text='using new line \n for this long text').grid(column=0,row=4)
30
31        global myImage   #set this or use init, otherwise image lost to trash collection
32        myImage=PhotoImage(file='c:/python33/lib/idlelib/icons/python.gif')
33        Label(root,image=myImage, style='myLabel.TLabel').grid(column=0,row=5)
34
35        #add a button to change variable text in the label
36        Button(root,text='Press Me', command=Pressed).grid(column=0,row=6)
37        Label(root,textvariable=myText,background='pink',width=20).grid(column=1,row=6)
38
39        global myBitMap
40        myBitMap = BitmapImage(file='c:/python33/tcl/tk8.5/demos/images/face.xbm')
41        Label(root,image=myBitMap).grid(column=1,row=7)
42    def Pressed():
43        if myText.get()=='YES':
44            myText.set('NO')
45        else:
46            myText.set('YES')
47
48    if __name__=="__main__":
49        root = Tk()
50        root.title("RyMax Window on the world")
51        root.geometry("470x420+200+10")#width, height, x location, y location
52        myText=StringVar()
53        myText.set('YES')
54        label()
55        root.mainloop()
```

Text 34: Label2

Frame and Label Frame for Widget Placement

As we add more widgets to the GUI you can see that placement is becoming a major issue. I am going to continue using the 'grid' geometry manager for widget placement. You may find that using 'pack' or 'place' as your Tkinter geometry manager to be more to your liking. Whichever you choose do not mix them in the same program as they may conflict on placing the widget

As we expand our presentations the use of Frames on the window makes life a heck of a lot easier. As our previous program had a fair number of widgets we will use that to program to build our Frame and Label Frame Example. I generally like to use the LabelFrame vs. the Frame so there is only one Frame included in the sample, but the two work pretty much the same.

First, we did this instruction on two lines. This makes it easier to read in the program and sometimes I have found some widgets want to be defined in this manner vs. on one line. I don't like exceptions just make it a rule to break things out until you are comfortable. A description of our first Label Frame is shown in the following.

  myFrame = LabelFrame (root, text="My Label Frame", width=100, height=100):
- myFrame is the name of this LabelFrame
- LabelFrame is the tkinter widget name
- root is the window we want to place the LabelFrame in

- text is the title of the frame
- width and height are the size of the frame in pixels

myFrame.grid(column=0, row=0):

- myFrame.grid is the positioning feature of myFrame
- column=0 tells the program to position the LabelFrame in column 0 of the root window
- row=0 tells the program to position the LabelFrame in row 0 of the root window. Remember the column=0 and row=0 will start this LabelFrame in the top left hand corner of the root window.
- Try some different sizes and check the results.

You may have noticed that the width and height do not seem to apply, and you are correct. The Label Frame without explicit instruction will size itself to hold the contents placed in it. You may also have noticed that the My Label Frame is centered on row 0. In order to control the placement of the Label Frame we can use those 'sticky' options you have seen in some of the other programs. When we define My Third Label Frame some sticky values are included. In this case we slid the Frame over to the left or west; by using the 'W' designator.

If we want the Label Frame to fill the size that we specify we need to instruct the grid manager to in effect stretch our Label Frame. We do that with sticky=('nsew'). This stretches the Label Frame in four directions to fill the size we specified.

The grid manager is probably one of the simplest layout tools, but it needs you to understand a number of things. Grid manager thinks in terms of columns and rows within the window or frame. Columns and rows start with 0 in the top left hand corner of the frame or window. Grid manager will expand as needed based on your 'sticky' instructions. But it wants to conserve space and not take more than it needs to display your widgets. It can give you some results you probably would never expect. I think you can see how easy it is to move widgets around.

I have also included a 'Frame Widget', really very similar to the 'Label Frame Widget' without the text name option.

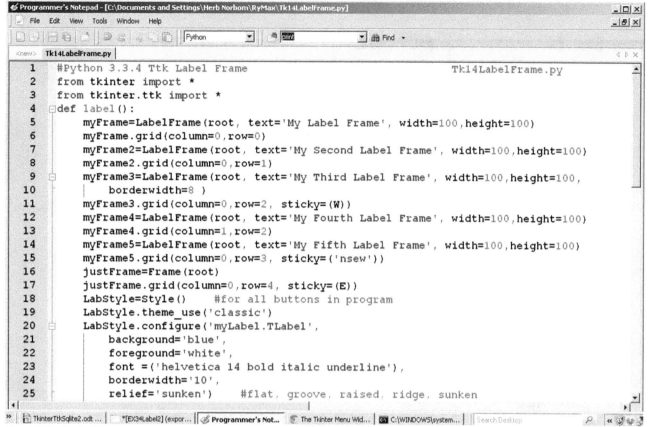

```
    1    #Python 3.3.4 Ttk Label Frame                    Tk14LabelFrame.py
    2    from tkinter import *
    3    from tkinter.ttk import *
    4    def label():
    5        myFrame=LabelFrame(root, text='My Label Frame', width=100,height=100)
    6        myFrame.grid(column=0,row=0)
    7        myFrame2=LabelFrame(root, text='My Second Label Frame', width=100,height=100)
    8        myFrame2.grid(column=0,row=1)
    9        myFrame3=LabelFrame(root, text='My Third Label Frame', width=100,height=100,
   10            borderwidth=8 )
   11        myFrame3.grid(column=0,row=2, sticky=(W))
   12        myFrame4=LabelFrame(root, text='My Fourth Label Frame', width=100,height=100)
   13        myFrame4.grid(column=1,row=2)
   14        myFrame5=LabelFrame(root, text='My Fifth Label Frame', width=100,height=100)
   15        myFrame5.grid(column=0,row=3, sticky=('nsew'))
   16        justFrame=Frame(root)
   17        justFrame.grid(column=0,row=4, sticky=(E))
   18        LabStyle=Style()        #for all buttons in program
   19        LabStyle.theme_use('classic')
   20        LabStyle.configure('myLabel.TLabel',
   21            background='blue',
   22            foreground='white',
   23            font =('helvetica 14 bold italic underline'),
   24            borderwidth='10',
   25            relief='sunken')        #flat, groove, raised, ridge, sunken
```

Text 35: LabelFrame

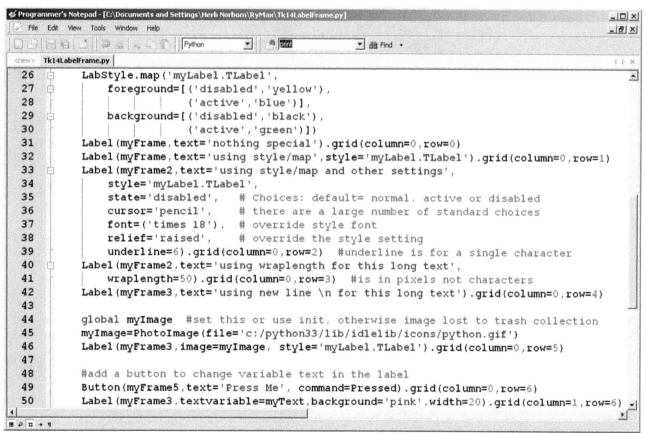

```
   26        LabStyle.map('myLabel.TLabel',
   27            foreground=[('disabled','yellow'),
   28                        ('active','blue')],
   29            background=[('disabled','black'),
   30                        ('active','green')])
   31        Label(myFrame,text='nothing special').grid(column=0,row=0)
   32        Label(myFrame,text='using style/map',style='myLabel.TLabel').grid(column=0,row=1)
   33        Label(myFrame2,text='using style/map and other settings',
   34            style='myLabel.TLabel',
   35            state='disabled',    # Choices: default= normal, active or disabled
   36            cursor='pencil',     # there are a large number of standard choices
   37            font=('times 18'),   # override style font
   38            relief='raised',     # override the style setting
   39            underline=6).grid(column=0,row=2)  #underline is for a single character
   40        Label(myFrame2,text='using wraplength for this long text',
   41            wraplength=50).grid(column=0,row=3)  #is in pixels not characters
   42        Label(myFrame3,text='using new line \n for this long text').grid(column=0,row=4)
   43
   44        global myImage  #set this or use init, otherwise image lost to trash collection
   45        myImage=PhotoImage(file='c:/python33/lib/idlelib/icons/python.gif')
   46        Label(myFrame3,image=myImage, style='myLabel.TLabel').grid(column=0,row=5)
   47
   48        #add a button to change variable text in the label
   49        Button(myFrame5,text='Press Me', command=Pressed).grid(column=0,row=6)
   50        Label(myFrame3,textvariable=myText,background='pink',width=20).grid(column=1,row=6)
```

Text 36: LabelFrame2

```
51
52          global myBitMap
53          myBitMap = BitmapImage(file='c:/python33/tcl/tk8.5/demos/images/face.xbm')
54          Label(myFrame4,image=myBitMap).grid(column=1,row=7)
55
56          Label(justFrame, text='inside a plain Frame').grid(column=0,row=0)
57  def Pressed():
58      if myText.get()=='YES':
59          myText.set('NO')
60      else:
61          myText.set('YES')
62
63  if __name__=="__main__":
64      root = Tk()
65      root.title("RyMax Window on the world")
66      root.geometry("470x450+200+10")#width, height, x location, y location
67      myText=StringVar()
68      myText.set('YES')
69      label()
70      root.mainloop()
```

Text 37: LabelFrame3

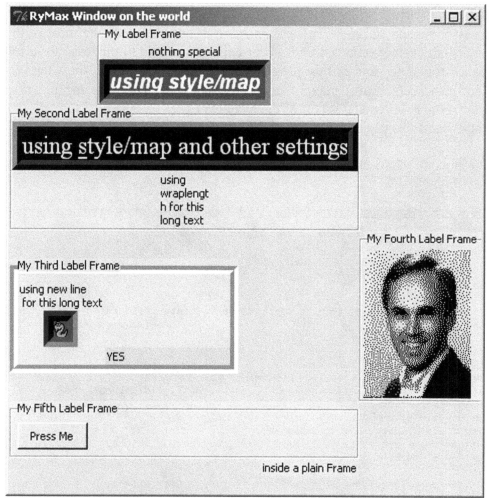

Text 38: LabelFrameResults

Menu System

Python has a very nice pull down menu system via Tkinter. As you get into it I am sure you will see some familiarity to whatever system you currently use. Setup the pull down menu by adding a very small amount of code to a program. When we run this program note the new items near the top of the window.

There are a lot of features in this program besides the menu system. Why have a menu unless it does something, so I added a bunch of items that you may like to play with. First we expanded our import list and second a number of procedures have been added. We will call or run these procedures when we click menu items.

Listbox, checkbutton, and radiobutton in Menu

The menu code starts on line 84, line by line explanation follows.

- menubar = Menu(root) – build a menu in the root window and call the Menu 'menubar'
- filemenu = Menu (menu=menubar, tearoff=0) –this begins the construction of our menu categories. The tearoff has do with putting a dotted tear off line, if you leave at 0 no dotted line, change to a 1 and you will see the dotted line. There are a number of options, for this purpose we are just scratching the surface. If you add a tearoff, click on the dotted line and the menu is shown separately.
- filemenu.add_separator() – this adds a separator line between the item, try commenting this line out

and rerun the program
- filemenu.add_command (label="Exit", command=root.quit) – this is the meat of the menu structure where you actually can execute a command or call a function. In this case we are just going to call the command root.quit and exit the program. Added some font fun to show the versatility.
- Menubar.add_cascade(menu=filemenu, label='File') – this adds the menu category File to the filemenu, and note the filemenu is part of the menubar

As we add additional items this should become a little clearer.

I have included the capability to create a <u>new</u> file, be careful as you can easily destroy an existing file.

```python
#Python 3.3.4 Ttk Menu  with Listbox, checkbutton, radiobutton        Tk15Menu.py
from tkinter import *
from tkinter.ttk import *
import tkinter.messagebox, tkinter.simpledialog, tkinter.filedialog,tkinter.colorchooser
def newFile():
    global Entry1, TOP
    TOP=Toplevel()
    TOP.title("RyMax New File Window")
    TOP.geometry("300x150+525+100") #width, height, x location, y location
    Label(TOP,text='Enter file name and press Enter').grid(column=1,row=0)
    Entry1=Entry(TOP)
    Entry1.grid(column=0,row=0)
    Entry1.bind("<Return>", createFile)
    Button(TOP, text='Press to close Window',command=TOP.destroy).grid(column=0,row=4)
def createFile(event):
    try:
        f = open(Entry1.get(),'r')  #test to see if file exists
        resp=tkinter.messagebox.askyesno(message='File Exists, this destroys old file',
            icon='question', title='Are you Sure?')
        if resp == True:
            f= open(Entry1.get(),'w')
            Label(TOP,text='File Deleted and Created').grid(column=1,row=2)
        else:
            Label(TOP,text='NO ACTION TAKEN').grid(column=1,row=2)
            return
    except:             # file doesn't exist so create it
        f = open(Entry1.get(),'w')
        Label(TOP,text='File Created').grid(column=1,row=2)
```

Text 39: Menu Program

```python
29  def openFile():
30      filename = tkinter.filedialog.askopenfilename()
31      print ('File Selected to open: ',filename)
32      #you need to add instructions for what progam to use to open file
33  def changeDirectory():
34      dirname = tkinter.filedialog.askdirectory()
35      print ('Directory choosen: ',dirname)    #only valid in this procedure
36  def chooseColor():
37      colorSel=tkinter.colorchooser.askcolor(initialcolor='#ff0000')
38      print (colorSel)
39  def messageToday(): tkinter.messagebox.showinfo(message='Yor are really smart!')
40  def showPythonVersion():
41      pyVersion=sys.version
42      tkinter.messagebox.showwarning('Python Version',pyVersion)
43  def showSystemPlatform():
44      import platform
45      osType=platform.system()
46      osPlatform=platform.win32_ver()
47      osProcessor=platform.processor()
48      tkinter.messagebox.showwarning('System Information','Operating System: '+ osType +
49          '\nSystem Info:'+osPlatform[0]+
50          '\nRelease: '+osPlatform[1]+
51          '\nService Pack: '+ osPlatform[2]+
52          '\nMultiProcessor: '+osPlatform[3]+
53          '\nProcessor: ' + osProcessor)
54  def searchPaths():
55      searchWin=Toplevel()
56      searchFrame = LabelFrame(searchWin,text="Python Search Paths", width =100, height=10)
```

Text 40: Menu Program2

```python
57        searchFrame.grid(column=0, row=0, sticky =NW)
58        searchBox=Listbox(searchFrame, width=150,height=10)
59        searchBox.grid(column=0, row=0,sticky=NW)
60        scrollBar = Scrollbar(searchFrame, orient=VERTICAL, command=searchBox.yview)
61        scrollBar.grid(column=1, row=0,sticky=(N,W,E,S))
62        searchBox['yscrollcommand']=scrollBar.set
63        myPythonSearch=[]
64        for folder in sys.path:
65            print (folder)
66            myPythonSearch.append (folder)
67        for item in myPythonSearch:
68            searchBox.insert('end',item)
69    def checkButtonV():
70        print (checkValue.get())
71    def ckRadioV():
72        print (radioValue.get())
73    def showRyMax():
74        tkinter.messagebox.showwarning('RyMax, Inc.','RyMax, Inc.'+
75            '\n e-mail: herb@rymax.biz')
76    def currentDirectory():
77        tkinter.messagebox.showinfo('RyMax Current Folder','Current Folder is: '+sys.path[0])
78
79    if __name__=="__main__":
80        root = Tk()
81        root.title("RyMax Window on the world")
82        root.geometry("300x100+200+10")#width, height, x location, y location
83
84        menubar = Menu(root)
```

Text 41: Menu Program3

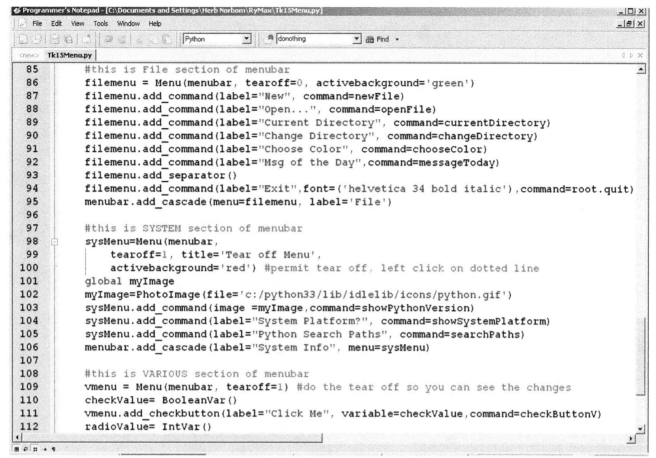

```
85        #this is File section of menubar
86        filemenu = Menu(menubar, tearoff=0, activebackground='green')
87        filemenu.add_command(label="New", command=newFile)
88        filemenu.add_command(label="Open...", command=openFile)
89        filemenu.add_command(label="Current Directory", command=currentDirectory)
90        filemenu.add_command(label="Change Directory", command=changeDirectory)
91        filemenu.add_command(label="Choose Color", command=chooseColor)
92        filemenu.add_command(label="Msg of the Day",command=messageToday)
93        filemenu.add_separator()
94        filemenu.add_command(label="Exit",font=('helvetica 34 bold italic'),command=root.quit)
95        menubar.add_cascade(menu=filemenu, label='File')
96
97        #this is SYSTEM section of menubar
98        sysMenu=Menu(menubar,
99            tearoff=1, title='Tear off Menu',
100           activebackground='red') #permit tear off, left click on dotted line
101       global myImage
102       myImage=PhotoImage(file='c:/python33/lib/idlelib/icons/python.gif')
103       sysMenu.add_command(image =myImage,command=showPythonVersion)
104       sysMenu.add_command(label="System Platform?", command=showSystemPlatform)
105       sysMenu.add_command(label="Python Search Paths", command=searchPaths)
106       menubar.add_cascade(label="System Info", menu=sysMenu)
107
108       #this is VARIOUS section of menubar
109       vmenu = Menu(menubar, tearoff=1) #do the tear off so you can see the changes
110       checkValue= BooleanVar()
111       vmenu.add_checkbutton(label="Click Me", variable=checkValue,command=checkButtonV)
112       radioValue= IntVar()
```

Text 42: Menu Program4

There are a lot of possible screen displays when running the program. I have grouped a number of them in the results display.

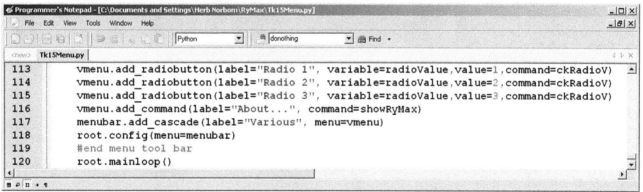

```
113       vmenu.add_radiobutton(label="Radio 1", variable=radioValue,value=1,command=ckRadioV)
114       vmenu.add_radiobutton(label="Radio 2", variable=radioValue,value=2,command=ckRadioV)
115       vmenu.add_radiobutton(label="Radio 3", variable=radioValue,value=3,command=ckRadioV)
116       vmenu.add_command(label="About...", command=showRyMax)
117       menubar.add_cascade(label="Various", menu=vmenu)
118       root.config(menu=menubar)
119       #end menu tool bar
120       root.mainloop()
```

Text 43: Menu Program5

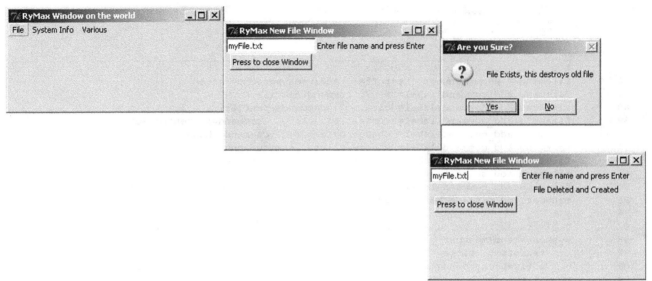

Text 44: Menu File New

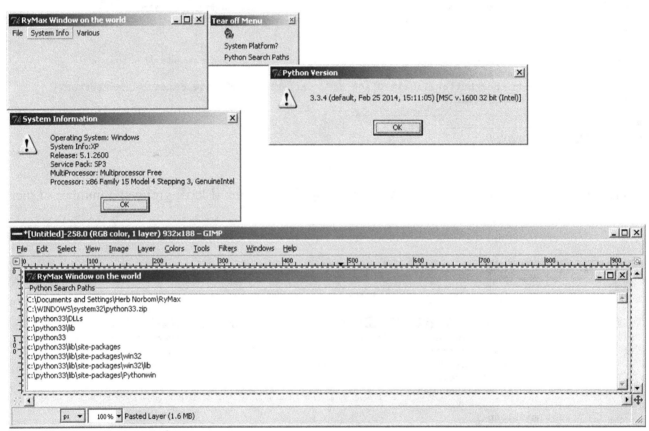

Text 45: Menu System Info

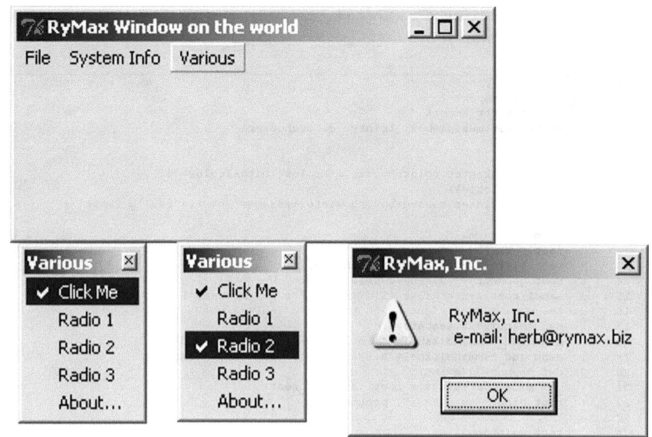

Text 46: Menu Various

Popup Menu

Another nice feature is the ability to add a popup menu to your programs. Works similar to our previous menu program only here we bind to the Right Mouse Button. I made this a tear off menu as it is easier to make the exhibits, you may want to use 'tearoff=0'.

```
1    #Python 3.3.4 Ttk Popup Menu                          Tk16PopupMenu.py
2    from tkinter import *
3    from tkinter.ttk import *
4    import tkinter.messagebox, tkinter.colorchooser
5
6    def cmd1():
7        colorSel=tkinter.colorchooser.askcolor(initialcolor='#ff0000')
8        print (colorSel)
9    def cmd2(): tkinter.messagebox.showinfo(message='Yor are really smart!')
10
11   if __name__=="__main__":
12       root = Tk()
13       root.title("RyMax Window on the world")
14       root.geometry("300x100+200+10")#width, height, x location, y location
15       Label(root,text='Right Click Mouse for Pop Up Menu').grid(column=1,row=0)
16       #popup section   right click on mouse displays menu
17       menu=Menu(root,tearoff=1)
18       menu.add_command(label='Color Choice', command = cmd1)
19       menu.add_command(label='Message Today', command = cmd2)
20       def popupMenu(event):
21           menu.post(event.x_root, event.y_root)
22       root.bind("<Button-3>", popupMenu)
23
24       root.mainloop()
```

Text 47: Popup Menu

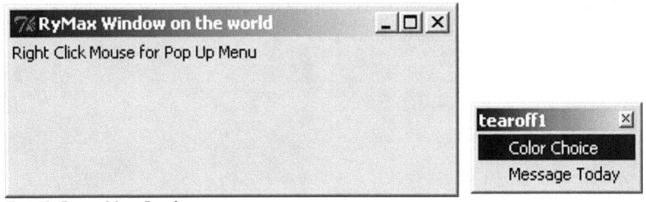

Text 48: Popup Menu Result

Message Boxes

As we have seen in previous programs these standard message boxes are very easy to use and good for notifying the user of events and gathering simple replies. The following demonstrates some of the features.

Note near end of program we open a second window to demonstrate the creation of our own messaging display. You may need to create your own when you are not happy with the standard buttons.

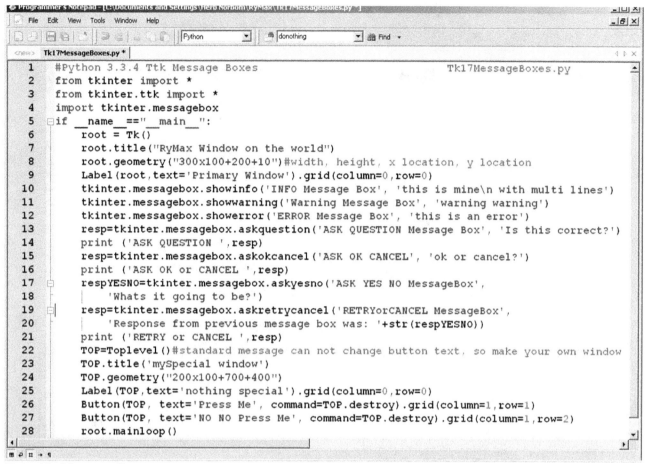

```python
1   #Python 3.3.4 Ttk Message Boxes                         Tk17MessageBoxes.py
2   from tkinter import *
3   from tkinter.ttk import *
4   import tkinter.messagebox
5   if __name__=="__main__":
6       root = Tk()
7       root.title("RyMax Window on the world")
8       root.geometry("300x100+200+10")#width, height, x location, y location
9       Label(root,text='Primary Window').grid(column=0,row=0)
10      tkinter.messagebox.showinfo('INFO Message Box', 'this is mine\n with multi lines')
11      tkinter.messagebox.showwarning('Warning Message Box', 'warning warning')
12      tkinter.messagebox.showerror('ERROR Message Box', 'this is an error')
13      resp=tkinter.messagebox.askquestion('ASK QUESTION Message Box', 'Is this correct?')
14      print ('ASK QUESTION ',resp)
15      resp=tkinter.messagebox.askokcancel('ASK OK CANCEL', 'ok or cancel?')
16      print ('ASK OK or CANCEL ',resp)
17      respYESNO=tkinter.messagebox.askyesno('ASK YES NO MessageBox',
18          'Whats it going to be?')
19      resp=tkinter.messagebox.askretrycancel('RETRYorCANCEL MessageBox',
20          'Response from previous message box was: '+str(respYESNO))
21      print ('RETRY or CANCEL ',resp)
22      TOP=Toplevel()#standard message can not change button text, so make your own window
23      TOP.title('mySpecial window')
24      TOP.geometry("200x100+700+400")
25      Label(TOP,text='nothing special').grid(column=0,row=0)
26      Button(TOP, text='Press Me', command=TOP.destroy).grid(column=1,row=1)
27      Button(TOP, text='NO NO Press Me', command=TOP.destroy).grid(column=1,row=2)
28      root.mainloop()
```

Text 49: Message Box

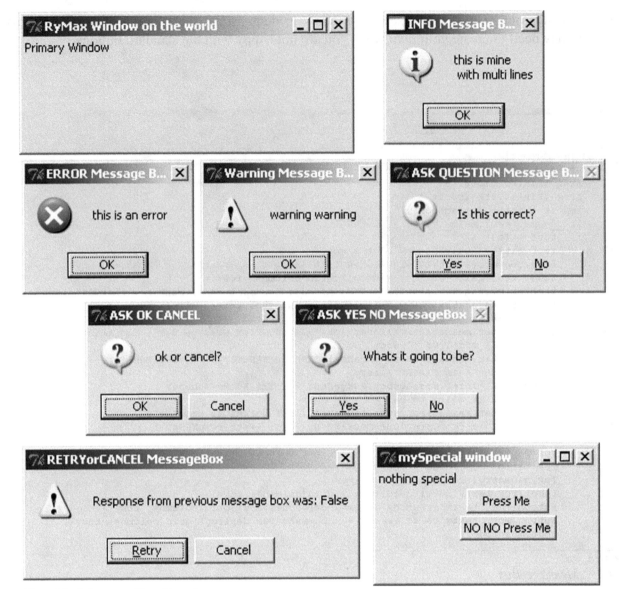

Text 50: Message Box Results

More Widget Placement, Remove, Forget, Compound and Sizegrip

As we have a number of widgets to work with we will expand on our placement options for widgets. As we had a number of widgets in our 'Tk14LabelFrame.py' program I am going to rename that to 'Tk18WidgetPlacement.py' for a starting point and then I made a number of changes.

The programs most significant changes are related to the procedures defined by our Button Command. I used the Button to trigger the 'remove' and 'forget' grid functions. Other changes are sprinkled about the widgets and are mostly related to formatting. It seemed appropriate to include the 'gridinfo' at startup, however I do not expect to be using any of that information as I find it cryptic and really not sure why I would need to use it.

Sticky and Anchor

Examples of 'anchor', 'sticky' and 'justify' are included, but a little discussion is in order. 'Sticky' is used to paste your widget in whatever you define, example within a frame. Sticky values are 'n','s','e','w'. You can combine the directions, examples: 'ne', 'se'. The 'ne' makes your widget stick to the north and east side of the container or frame. Using 'nsew', will stretch your widget to fill the container on all sides. The actual formatting of the sticky option is a little bit confusing. You can use for example: sticky=W or sticky='w', but sticky=w will not work. In other words if you use lower case enclose the directions in quotes, and if you use upper case directions you can skip the quotes or include them.

'Anchor' is for the text or data contained within the widget, and not for the widget itself. In this program it is used on the 'Label' widget. The choices are (n, ne, e, se, s, sw, w, nw or center) they must be enclosed in quotes. OR, you can use capitals (N,NE,E,SE,SW,W,NW or CENTER)and not use quotes.

Justify
'Justify' is for alignment of text within the widget, for example in our Label. We can use (left, center, right) with quotes or (LEFT, CENTER, RIGHT) without quotes. This option is most useful for multiple lined text.

Compound for Text and Image
When you want to display an image and text use the 'compound' option. Valid options are: LEFT, CENTER, RIGHT or 'left', 'center', 'right'. See the Label in the 'justFrame' section. I could not get this to work with the bitmap image. Or more likely it worked just could not see it under the bitmap.

The program combines a lot of movement and option setting that you would probably not want to use in your program. This example as are the other examples just demonstrating various features. After you have the program running I suggest you play with the options to get a feel for just how powerful Tkinter/Ttk is.

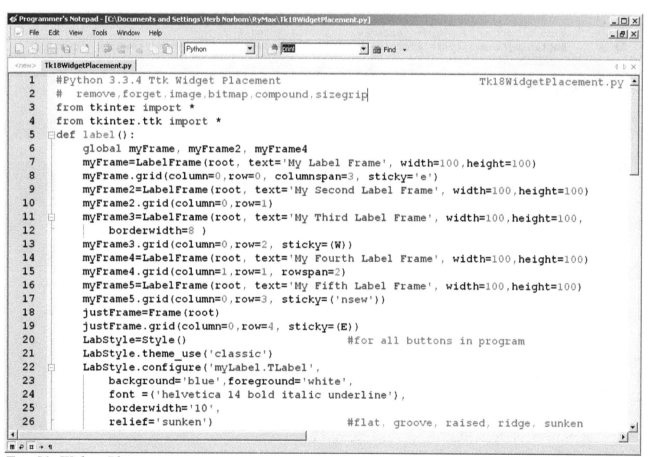

Text 51: Widget Placement

```
27    LabStyle.map('myLabel.TLabel',
28        foreground=[('disabled','yellow'),
29                    ('active','blue')],
30        background=[('disabled','black'),
31                    ('active','green')])
32    Label(myFrame,text='nothing special',width=25,anchor='e').grid(column=0,row=0)
33    Label(myFrame,text='using style/map',style='myLabel.TLabel').grid(column=0,row=1)
34    Label(myFrame2,text='using style/map and other settings',
35        style='myLabel.TLabel',
36        state='disabled',              # Choices: default= normal, active or disabled
37        cursor='pencil',               # there are many standard choices
38        font=('times 18'),             # override style font
39        relief='raised',               # override the style setting
40        underline=6).grid(column=0,row=2)    #underline is for a single character
41    Label(myFrame2,text='using wraplength & justify for this long text',
42        wraplength=150,                       #is in pixels not characters
43        anchor=E,
44        justify='center').grid(column=0,row=3)
45    Label(myFrame3,text='using new line \n for this long text').grid(column=0,row=4)
46
47    global myImage  #set this or use init, otherwise image lost to trash collection
48    myImage=PhotoImage(file='c:/python33/lib/idlelib/icons/python.gif')
49    Label(myFrame3,text='Hi there',
50        image=myImage,   style='myLabel.TLabel').grid(column=0,row=5)
51
52    #add a button to change variable text in the label
53    Button(myFrame5,text='Press Me', command=Pressed).grid(column=0,row=6)
```

Text 52: Widget Placement2

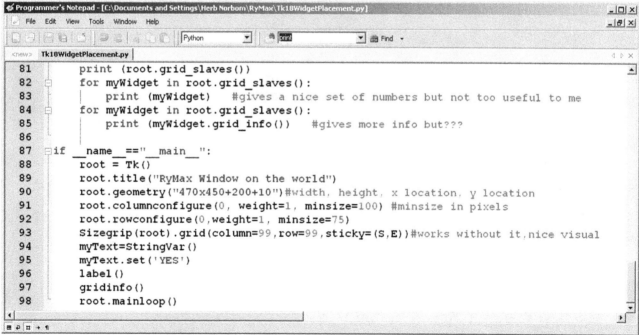

```
54         Label(myFrame3,textvariable=myText,background='pink',width=20,
55             relief='groove').grid(column=1,row=6)
56
57         global myBitMap
58         myBitMap = BitmapImage(file='c:/python33/tcl/tk8.5/demos/images/face.xbm')
59         Label(myFrame4,image=myBitMap).grid(column=1,row=7)
60
61         Label(justFrame,
62             compound='center',        # LEFT, CENTER, RIGHT,'left','center','right'
63             text='inside a plain Frame with padding',
64             image=myImage).grid(column=0,row=0,padx=5, pady=10)
65
66 def Pressed():
67         global myFrame2
68         if myText.get()=='YES':
69             myText.set('NO')
70             myFrame2.grid_forget()   #remove slave, specify grid postion to bring back
71             myFrame4.grid()          #as used 'remove' remembers the grid location
72             myFrame.grid_forget()
73             myFrame.grid(column=0, row=0)
74         else:
75             myText.set('YES')
76             myFrame2.grid(column=0,row=1)# need to get same postion back,try '.grid()'
77             myFrame4.grid_remove()
78             myFrame.grid_forget()
79             myFrame.grid(column=0, row=0,columnspan=3, sticky=E)
80 def gridinfo():
```

Text 53: Widget Placement3

```
81         print (root.grid_slaves())
82         for myWidget in root.grid_slaves():
83             print (myWidget)    #gives a nice set of numbers but not too useful to me
84         for myWidget in root.grid_slaves():
85             print (myWidget.grid_info())    #gives more info but???
86
87 if __name__=="__main__":
88         root = Tk()
89         root.title("RyMax Window on the world")
90         root.geometry("470x450+200+10")#width, height, x location, y location
91         root.columnconfigure(0, weight=1, minsize=100) #minsize in pixels
92         root.rowconfigure(0,weight=1, minsize=75)
93         Sizegrip(root).grid(column=99,row=99,sticky=(S,E))#works without it,nice visual
94         myText=StringVar()
95         myText.set('YES')
96         label()
97         gridinfo()
98         root.mainloop()
```

Text 54: Widget Placement4

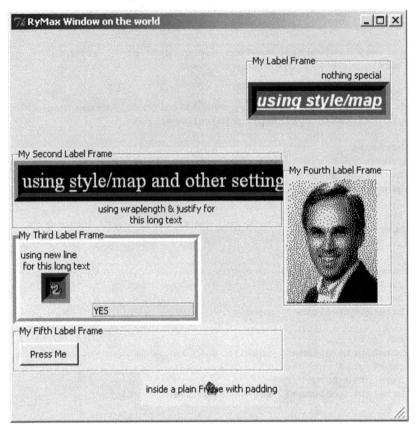

Text 55: Widget Placement Result

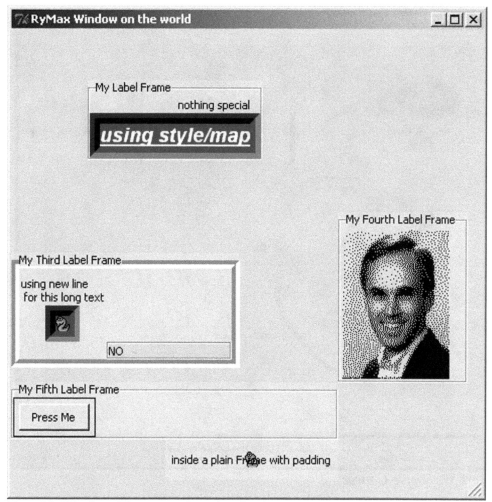

Text 56: Window Placement Result after button press once

Press the button several times and notice the changes. Also use the size grip, in particular when you are shrinking the window, notice how the minimum size comes into play.

Canvas

The canvas widget can be a lot of fun for your drawings and developing games. For now we will develop a simple Tkinter Canvas that includes some basic shapes and the ability to draw. While this program is basic it is amazing what can be accomplished in twenty eight lines of code. The display which follows includes a quick scribble made while dragging the mouse. The shapes and image are pretty easy to add.

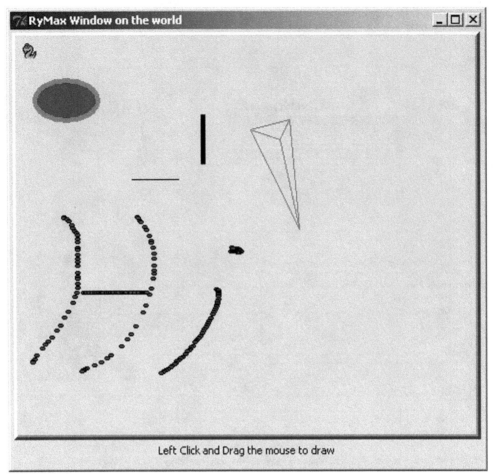

Text 57: Simple Canvas

As you look at this and hopefully play with the code you will quickly want to change the brush, the colors, etc. Not to mention save or print your product. In the Appendices I have included a fairly comprehensive program that lets you accomplish a pretty fair amount. That program is considerably larger. If you are not into entering the entire program look at it for features that you may want. When it comes to saving your Canvas I have found the best way is saving to a postscript file. I then read the file using 'Gimp', but you can use what you like that reads 'ps' files. One drawback that I have not figured out a good way around is in saving my canvas and being able to reload it at some future time. The closest I have come is saving as a postscript, reading the file into Gimp and exporting out of Gimp as a 'GIF', and then finally importing the GIF image back into the Canvas. Hopefully you will find a better method if you need that capability.

The following is the simple Canvas program, good for doodling and a quick start into the shallow end of the Canvas pool.

```python
1    #Python 3.3.4 Ttk Canvas                          Tk18Canvas.py
2    from tkinter import *
3    from tkinter.ttk import *
4    class setupCanvas:
5        def __init__(self):
6            self.Canvas=Canvas(root,width =475,height=400,borderwidth=5,relief=RAISED)
7            self.Canvas.grid(column=0, row=0)
8            self.Canvas.configure(cursor="crosshair")
9            self.Canvas.bind( "<B1-Motion>", self.paint )
10           Label(root,text="Left Click and Drag the mouse to draw").grid(column=0,row=3)
11           self.myImage=PhotoImage(file='c:/python33/lib/idlelib/icons/python.gif')
12           self.Canvas.create_line(125,150,175,150,width=1)#horizontal start(125,150)end(175,150)
13           self.Canvas.create_line(200,85,200,135,width=5) #vertical start(200,85) end(200,135)
14           self.Canvas.create_oval(25,50,90,90,width=5,fill='blue',outline='red',activefill='tan')
15           p1= (300,200)        #bottom common point for a Tetrahedron
16           p2= (250,100)        #top left front
17           p3= (280,110)        #top right front
18           p4= (290,90)         #triangle to right side
19           self.Canvas.create_polygon(p1,p2,p3,p1,p4,p3,p2,p4,fill='',width=1,outline='red')
20           self.Canvas.create_image(20,20,image=self.myImage)
21       def paint( self, event ):
22           self.Canvas.create_oval(event.x, event.y,event.x+5, event.y+3,fill='blue')
23   if __name__=='__main__':
24       root = Tk()
25       root.title( "RyMax Window on the world" )
26       root.geometry( "490x440+50+30" ) #width, height, placement y  x
27       setupCanvas()
28       mainloop()
```

Text 58: Simple Canvas

The following gives you an idea of what the Advanced Canvas program display looks like, it would be a complete separate book to adequately describe and demonstrate all the features available to the Canvas Widget. As you look at the Advanced display and program (In the Appendix) I hope you will notice how items we have already covered can be used to enhance the visual effects.

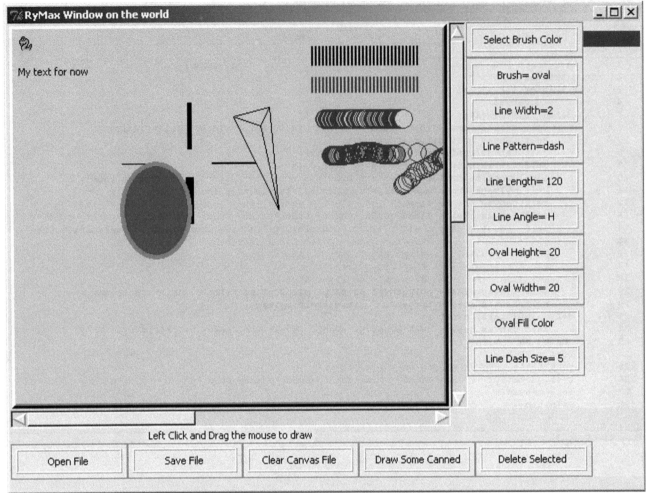

Text 59: Advanced Canvas Widget

Listbox

In our Menu program we used a Listbox but did not go into a lot of depth. Let's expand our Listbox and explore some of the features and uses. This widget lets you list lines of text, you will be able to scroll through the list and select a row from the list. You can only use one font, and no images. While our example program will only allow you to select one row at a time there are other options. 'Selectmode' can be: SINGLE, BROWSE(single with mouse use),MULTIPLE, EXTENDED(use of shift and control key to get multiple rows). I have just used the 'SINGLE' in our sample as you will get index errors when displaying the row selected if you used MULTIPLE or EXTENDED. Your insert and or delete actions only impact the ListBox and not the directory we are using. You may have noticed in Tkinter/Ttk for many of the widget options you can use CAPITAL letters or enclose the option in quotes, for example 'single' vs. SINGLE.

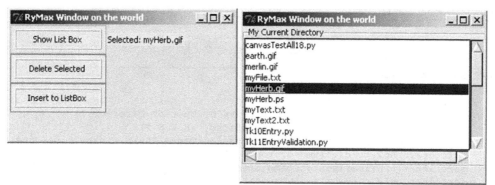

Text 60: ListBox

```
1   #Python 3.3.4  Listbox                              Tk20ListBox.py
2   from tkinter import *
3   from tkinter.ttk import *
4   import os
5   class setup:
6       def __init__(self):
7           self.BT=Style()
8           self.BT.theme_use('classic')
9           self.BT.configure('TButton')
10          self.BT.map('TButton',
11              foreground=[('disabled','yellow'),('pressed','red'),('active','blue')],
12              background=[('disabled','magenta'),('pressed','cyan'),('active','green')],
13              highlightcolor=[('focus','green'),('!focus','red')],
14              relief=[('pressed', 'groove'),('!pressed', 'ridge')])
15          self.B1=Button(root,text='Show List Box',width=15,
16              command=self.searchPaths,style='TButton').grid(column=0,row=0)
17          self.B2=Button(root,text='Delete Selected',width=15,
18              command=self.deleteSelected,style='TButton').grid(column=0,row=1)
19          self.B3=Button(root,text='Insert to ListBox',width=15,
20              command=self.insertText,style='TButton').grid(column=0,row=2)
```

Text 61: ListBox

```python
21      def searchPaths(self):
22          searchWin=Toplevel()
23          searchWin.geometry("325x200+300+190")#width, height, x location, y location
24          searchFrame=LabelFrame(searchWin,text="My Current Directory")
25          searchFrame.grid(column=0, row=0, sticky =(N,W,E,S))
26          self.searchBox=Listbox(searchFrame, selectmode=SINGLE,width=50,height=10)
27          self.searchBox.grid(column=0, row=0,sticky=NW)
28          scrollBar=Scrollbar(searchFrame,orient=VERTICAL,command=self.searchBox.yview)
29          scrollBar.grid(column=1, row=0,sticky=(N,S))
30          self.searchBox['yscrollcommand']=scrollBar.set
31          scrollBar=Scrollbar(searchFrame,orient=HORIZONTAL,command=self.searchBox.xview)
32          scrollBar.grid(column=0, row=1,sticky=(E,W))
33          self.searchBox['xscrollcommand']=scrollBar.set
34          fileList = os.listdir()      #gets the current directory files
35          for item in fileList:
36              self.searchBox.insert('end',item)
37          self.searchBox.bind('<ButtonRelease-1>', self.on_click_listbox)
38      def on_click_listbox(self, event):
39          index = self.searchBox.curselection()      # get selected line index
40          self.selectedFile = self.searchBox.get(index)      # get the line's text
```

Text 62: ListBox2

```python
41              Label(root,text='Selected: '+self.selectedFile).grid(column=1,row=0,sticky=(E,W))
42      def deleteSelected(self):     #only deletes from ListBox, you would want to use
43          self.searchBox.delete('anchor') #error trapping in this procedure
44          Label(root,text='Deleted: '+self.selectedFile).grid(column=1,row=1)
45      def insertText(self):#only inserts to ListBox, you would want to use error trap
46          Label(root,text='Press Return to Add').grid(column=1,row=3,sticky=(E,W))
47          self.myInput=''
48          self.Entry1=Entry(root)
49          self.Entry1.insert(0,self.myInput)
50          self.Entry1.grid(column=1,row=2)
51          self.Entry1.focus()
52          self.Entry1.bind("<Return>", self.addListBox)
53      def addListBox(self,event):
54          self.searchBox.insert(END,self.Entry1.get()) #error trapping in this procedure
55  if __name__=="__main__":
56      root = Tk()
57      root.title("RyMax Window on the world")
58      root.geometry("300x150+200+10")#width, height, x location, y location
59      setup()
60      root.mainloop()
```

Text 63: Listbox3

PanedWindow

I generally like to use the LabelFrame vs. the PanedWindow as I rarely have cause for the user to change the size of frames. For those special occasions where you need adjusting windows within a window this may be exactly what you want. Our version of Tkinter/Ttk uses the 'Style' option. A number of options from prior versions have not been carried forward, at least not that I could get to work. My example includes a number of 'do nothing buttons', just there to help you see the panes. The little 'blocks' between panes are for adjusting the pane size. Some of the panes use the 'Style' and two do not. I could not get the 'ridge' option to work with 'Style', I guess it is a default. At this point I would probably not use the 'Style' option at all. However in the future it may have more options.

```python
#Python 3.3.4   Paned Window                    Tk21PanedWindow.py
from tkinter import *
from tkinter.ttk import *
class setup:
    def __init__(s):      #a bunch of do nothing buttons
        s.B1=Button(pane1,text='PANE 1 BUTTON',width=15).grid(column=0,row=0)
        s.B2=Button(pane2,text='PANE 2 BUTTON',width=15).grid(column=0,row=1)
        s.B2=Button(pane2,text='PANE 2 BUTTON2',width=15).grid(column=0,row=2)
        s.B3=Button(pane3,text='PANE 3 BUTTON',width=15).grid(column=0,row=2)
        s.B4=Button(pane4,text='PANE 4 BUTTON',width=15).grid(column=0,row=0)
        s.B5=Button(pane5,text='PANE 5 BUTTON',width=15).grid(column=0,row=1)
        s.B5=Button(pane5,text='PANE 5 BUTTON2',width=15).grid(column=0,row=2)
        s.B6=Button(pane6,text='PANE 6 BUTTON',width=15).grid(column=0,row=2)
if __name__=="__main__":
    root = Tk()
    root.title("RyMax Window on the world")
    root.geometry("500x450+200+10")#width, height, x location, y location
    style=Style()
    style.theme_use('classic')
    style.configure("TPanedwindow")

    panedWin = Panedwindow(root, orient='horizontal')
    panedWin.config(height=100)
```

Text 64: PanedWindow

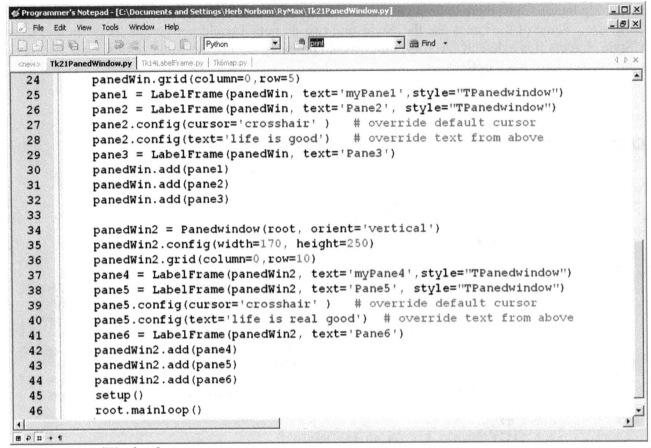

```
24    panedWin.grid(column=0,row=5)
25    pane1 = LabelFrame(panedWin, text='myPane1',style="TPanedwindow")
26    pane2 = LabelFrame(panedWin, text='Pane2', style="TPanedwindow")
27    pane2.config(cursor='crosshair' )   # override default cursor
28    pane2.config(text='life is good')   # override text from above
29    pane3 = LabelFrame(panedWin, text='Pane3')
30    panedWin.add(pane1)
31    panedWin.add(pane2)
32    panedWin.add(pane3)
33
34    panedWin2 = Panedwindow(root, orient='vertical')
35    panedWin2.config(width=170, height=250)
36    panedWin2.grid(column=0,row=10)
37    pane4 = LabelFrame(panedWin2, text='myPane4',style="TPanedwindow")
38    pane5 = LabelFrame(panedWin2, text='Pane5', style="TPanedwindow")
39    pane5.config(cursor='crosshair' )   # override default cursor
40    pane5.config(text='life is real good')  # override text from above
41    pane6 = LabelFrame(panedWin2, text='Pane6')
42    panedWin2.add(pane4)
43    panedWin2.add(pane5)
44    panedWin2.add(pane6)
45    setup()
46    root.mainloop()
```

Text 65: PanedWindow2

In the following you see the window as the program opens it, and using the size tabs, the closed panes.

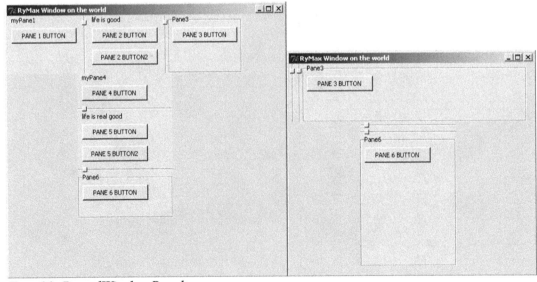

Text 66: PanedWindowResult

Option Menu

This is a great feature for giving the user a limited choice of values. Two Option Menu examples are included. In the first one the year values are defined in the Option Menu. The first option in the list is the one displayed in the Option Menu. In our example I included integer years and a string year. A string variable is required for the Option Menu.

In the second example a list of months are defined as a tuple, 'choices'. A string variable is needed and you can set a default value with the use of 'set'. The actual Option Menu uses the '*args' or in our case '*choices' to define or import our list of variables.

```python
#Python 3.3.4  OptionMenu                    Tk2OptionMenu.py
from tkinter import *
from tkinter.ttk import *

def getTheYear():
    L1=Label(root,  text=myOpt.get())
    L1.grid(column=2,row=0)
def getTheMonth():
    L1=Label(root,  text=myOptions.get())
    L1.grid(column=2,row=1)

if __name__=="__main__":
    root = Tk()
    root.title("RyMax Window on the world")
    root.geometry("300x150+200+10")#width, height, x location, y location
    myOpt = StringVar()
    OptionMenu(root, myOpt,2014,'2015',2016).grid(column=0, row=0)
    B1=Button(root,text='Press for Year', command=getTheYear)
    B1.grid(column=1, row=0)

    choices=["January","February","March",'APRIL',"MAY","JUNE",'JULY',
        'AUGUST','SEPTEMBER','OCTOBER','NOVEMBER','DECEMBER',999]
    myOptions = StringVar()
    myOptions.set(choices[0])
    OptionMenu(root, myOptions,*choices).grid(column=0, row=1)
    B1=Button(root,text='Press for Month', command=getTheMonth)
    B1.grid(column=1, row=1)
    root.mainloop()
```

Text 67: OptionMenu

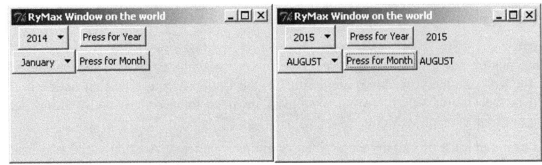

Text 68: OptionMenu Result

ComboBox

With this widget you can let your user enter values, you can use the validation routine we covered with the 'Entry Widget', and you can also set a default entry. In our program we take whatever the user enters or selects and when 'Return' is pressed we display a label with the results. If this was a new input we add it to the list.

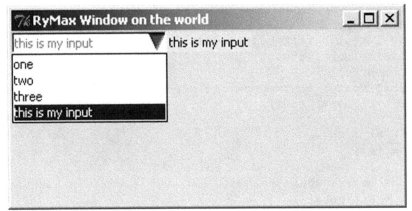

Text 69: ComboBox Result

```python
#Python 3.3.4   ComboBox                         Tk23ComboBox.py
from tkinter import *
from tkinter.ttk import *
class myComboBox():
    def __init__(self):
        self.myCombo = StringVar()
        self.myComboChoices =['one','two','three']
        self.myBox=Combobox(root,textvariable=self.myCombo,
            values=self.myComboChoices, style='TCombobox')
        self.myBox.grid(column=0, row=0)
        self.myBox.focus()
        self.myBox.bind('<Return>', self.handleit)
    def handleit(self,event):
        Label(root, text=self.myCombo.get()).grid(column=2,row=0, sticky=(E,W))
        self.myComboChoices.append(self.myCombo.get())
        self.myBox.configure(values=self.myComboChoices)
if __name__=="__main__":
    root = Tk()
    root.title("RyMax Window on the world")
    root.geometry("350x150+200+10")#width, height, x location, y location
    style=Style()
    style.theme_use('classic')
    style.configure('TCombobox',
        background='blue',foreground='red',relief='sunken')
    style.map('TCombobox',foreground=[('disabled','yellow'),('active','blue')],
        background=[('disabled','black'),('active','green')])
    myComboBox()
    root.mainloop()
```

Text 70: ComboBox

Spinbox

Another nice little feature, doesn't take up any screen space to speak of, yet gives the user a lot of choices. If you don't add too many choices it works best from a user perspective. In our example program we have three spins boxes. The first one has a range of -10 to 99 and as you use the arrow key or the slider the value increments by 5. When you press Return, the value you selected is displayed. Notice that the items are read only.

The next spinbox has three choices, but you can type in your own response also, when you press Return the label displays your input.

The third spinbox works like the second except we have used a 'lambda expression' in the command, and with that we print the value to the console. The 'lambda expression' is sometimes called the 'anonymous function'. As I am trying to concentrate on Tkinter/Ttk I am not going to explain 'lambda', just know it can be very useful. There is a fair amount of information on the web about it.

With the SpinBox you probably saw that I did not use the 'theme' or 'style'. At this point that is not available for this widget.

Tk22OptionMenu.py   **Tk24SpinBox.py**   Tk13Label.py

```python
1   #Python 3.3.4  Spinbox                        Tk24SpinBox.py
2   from tkinter import *
3   from tkinter.ttk import *
4   class mSBox():
5       def __init__(s):
6           s.mS = StringVar()
7           s.mS=Spinbox(root,textvariable=s.mS,from_=-10,to=99,increment=5,state='readonly')
8           s.mS.grid(column=0, row=0)
9           s.mS.bind('<Return>', s.handleit)
10          s.mS2 = StringVar()
11          s.mSChoices2 =['one','two','three']
12          s.mS2=Spinbox(root,textvariable=s.mS2,values=s.mSChoices2,relief='raised')
13          s.mS2.grid(column=0, row=1)
14          s.mS2.bind('<Return>', s.handleit2)
15          s.mS3 = StringVar()
16          s.mSChoices3 =['Jan','Feb','Mar']
17          s.mS3=Spinbox(root,textvariable=s.mS3,
18              values=s.mSChoices3,command=lambda: print(s.mS3.get()))
19          s.mS3.grid(column=0, row=2)
20      def handleit(s,event):Label(root,text=s.mS.get()).grid(column=2,row=0,sticky=(E,W))
21      def handleit2(s,event):Label(root,text=s.mS2.get()).grid(column=2,row=1,sticky=(E,W))
22  if __name__=="__main__":
23      root = Tk()
24      root.title("RyMax Window on the world")
25      root.geometry("350x50+200+10")#width, height, x location, y location
26      mSBox()
27      root.mainloop()
```

Text 71: SpinBox

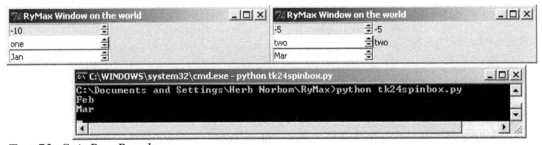

Text 72: SpinBox Result

Progressbar

If you want to keep your user informed about progress or just show the program is running while a long process is underway the Progressbar is your ticket. In our example I am just trying to show how it works, you would of course need to add some more useful code to adequately show a true progress. There are two 'modes' and this is a themed widget. The first mode is 'determinate', use this when you know the length of your process. The second mode is for when you just want to keep your user informed that the program is running but you do not know how long the process will take. In the program I have included the 'start' and 'stop' commands but neither is needed in this program, but you may need them.

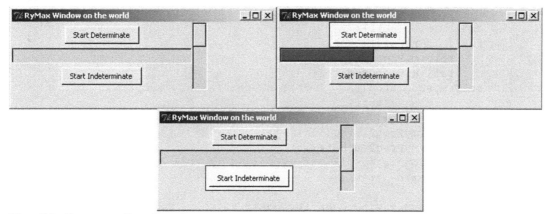

Text 73: Progress Bar Results

```
1   #Python 3.3.4   ProgressBar                    Tk25ProgressBar.py
2   from tkinter import *
3   from tkinter.ttk import *
4   class myProgressBar():
5       def __init__(self):
6           B1=Button(root,text='Start Determinate', command=self.determinate)
7           B1.grid(column=0, row=0)
8           self.myProg=Progressbar(root, orient=HORIZONTAL, length=275,
9               mode='determinate', style='Horizontal.TProgressbar')
10          self.myProg.start()              # in this case will work without it
11          self.myProg.grid(column=0, row=1)
12          self.myProg.config(maximum=1000000)
13          B2=Button(root,text='Start Indeterminate', command=self.indeterminate)
14          B2.grid(column=0, row=2)
15          self.myProg2=Progressbar(root, orient=VERTICAL, length=100,
16              mode='indeterminate', style='Vertical.TProgressbar')
17 #        self.myProg2.start()             # in this case will work without it
18          self.myProg2.grid(column=3, row=0,rowspan=4)
19          self.myProg2.config(maximum=1000000)
20
```

Text 74: ProgressBar

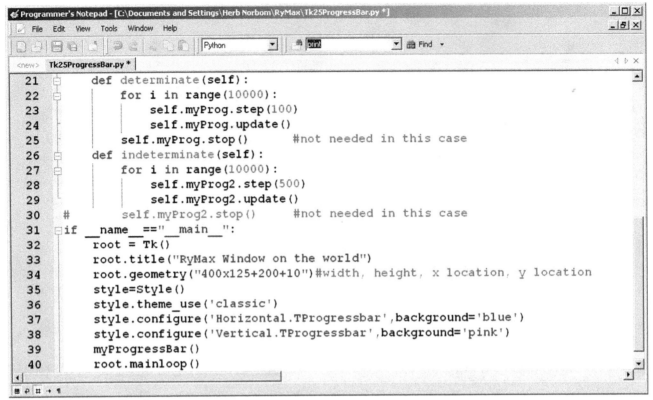

Text 75: ProgressBar2

Text

You will no doubt want to have the ability to add more than one line of input as provided for by the 'Entry' widget. The 'Text' widget will greatly assist you. While this widget is not part of the 'themed' widgets it is pretty powerful. I like to use the wrap=WORD and to not use the xScrollBar. If you want to use the xScrollBar I have found I have to set wrap=NONE.

You can highlight text and use the delete key. To copy and paste use CTRL C to copy and CTRL V to paste. To remove text you can also highlight the text and press CTRL X. There are many features to add for the Text Widget , you can basically make a fairly good word processor if you so desire.

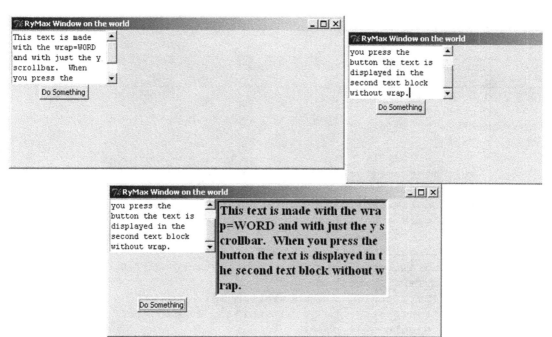

Text 76: Text Result

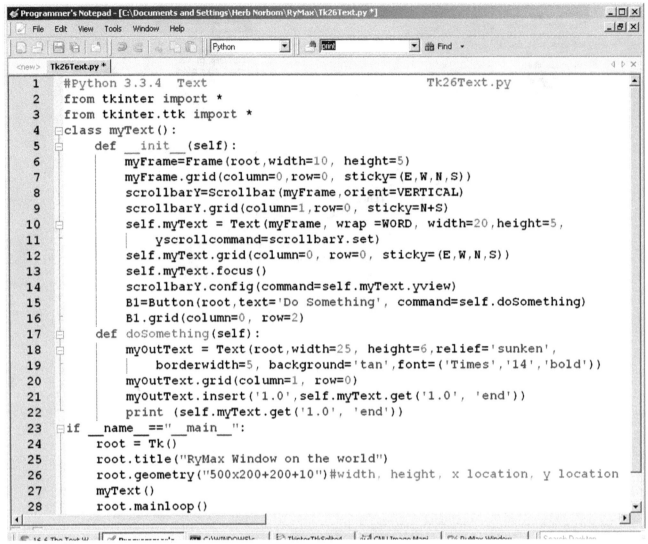

```
1   #Python 3.3.4  Text                      Tk26Text.py
2   from tkinter import *
3   from tkinter.ttk import *
4   class myText():
5       def __init__(self):
6           myFrame=Frame(root,width=10, height=5)
7           myFrame.grid(column=0,row=0, sticky=(E,W,N,S))
8           scrollbarY=Scrollbar(myFrame,orient=VERTICAL)
9           scrollbarY.grid(column=1,row=0, sticky=N+S)
10          self.myText = Text(myFrame, wrap =WORD, width=20,height=5,
11              yscrollcommand=scrollbarY.set)
12          self.myText.grid(column=0, row=0, sticky=(E,W,N,S))
13          self.myText.focus()
14          scrollbarY.config(command=self.myText.yview)
15          B1=Button(root,text='Do Something', command=self.doSomething)
16          B1.grid(column=0, row=2)
17      def doSomething(self):
18          myOutText = Text(root,width=25, height=6,relief='sunken',
19              borderwidth=5, background='tan',font=('Times','14','bold'))
20          myOutText.grid(column=1, row=0)
21          myOutText.insert('1.0',self.myText.get('1.0', 'end'))
22          print (self.myText.get('1.0', 'end'))
23  if __name__=="__main__":
24      root = Tk()
25      root.title("RyMax Window on the world")
26      root.geometry("500x200+200+10")#width, height, x location, y location
27      myText()
28      root.mainloop()
```

Text 77: Text

Scale

Scale is an interesting widget. It is now a themed widget, but it may have lost some features. Overall it is an improvement. Our example sets up a Horizontal and Vertical Scale. The Horizontal Scale used a double variable for its range(from_ and to). The '_' after from is required as 'from' is a reserved word. As you play with this notice if you click the mouse somewhere on the scale that the slider moves toward the mouse point.

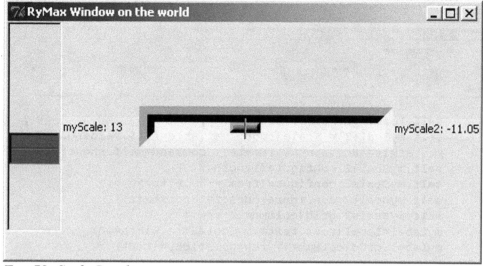

Text 78: Scale Result

```
                                                                    _|□|x|
 1    #Python 3.3.4  Scale                              Tk27Scale.py
 2    from tkinter import *
 3    from tkinter.ttk import *
 4   class myScale():
 5       def __init__(self):
 6           style=Style()
 7           style.theme_use('classic')
 8           style.configure("Vertical.TScale",
 9               background='blue',  foreground='white',
10               sliderrelief='sunken',  #default is raised which looks better
11               troughcolor='pink', sliderthickness=50)
12           style.configure("Horizontal.TScale",
13               background='red', borderwidth=15, #use default sliderrelief
14               troughcolor='yellow', sliderthickness=10)
15           style.map('Horizontal.TScale',
16           foreground=[('active','blue')],
17           background=[('active','green')])
18       #setup the Vertical Scale
19           self.reading=IntVar()
20           self.myScale = Scale(root, variable=self.reading,
21               style="Vertical.TScale", command=self.showIt)
22           self.myScale.configure(length=200)
23           self.myScale.configure(from_=-50,to=50)
24           self.myScale.configure(cursor='trek')
25           self.myScale.configure(orient=VERTICAL)
26           self.myScale.grid(column=0, row =0)
27           myLabel=Label(root,text='myScale: ',width=12)
28           myLabel.grid(column=2, row=0, sticky=(E+W))
```

Text 79: Scale

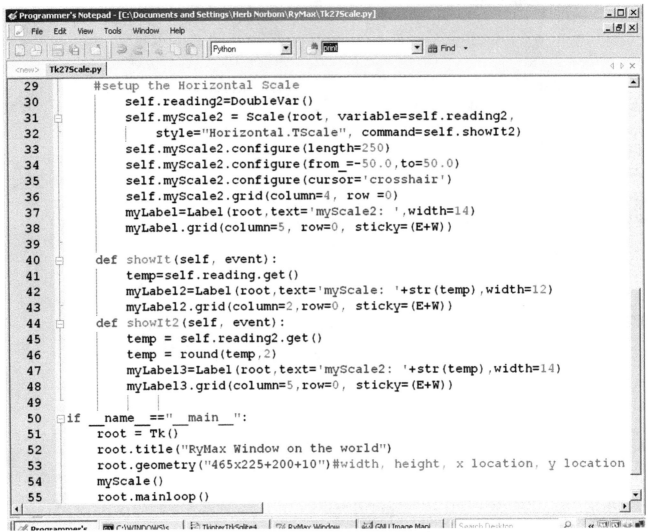

Text 80: Scale2

Radio Button

While we covered this to some extent in the Menu Program I wanted to go into more depth as it is a themed widget also. Notice the color changes as the cursor moves over the Radio Buttons. I have tried to use a number of different options for each button. When you press a RadioButton that button's value is displayed in the label.

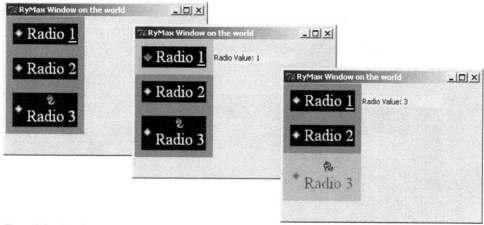

Text 81: RadioButton

```
1    #Python 3.3.4  Radio Buttons                      Tk28Radio.py
2    from tkinter import *
3    from tkinter.ttk import *
4    class myRadio():
5        def __init__(self):
6            style=Style()
7            style.theme_use('classic')
8            style.configure("TRadiobutton",background='black',foreground='white',font=('Times', '18'))
9            style.map('TRadiobutton',foreground=[('active','blue')],background=[('active','green')],
10               highlightcolor=[('focus','green'),('!focus','red')],
11               highlightthickness=[('!active',10),('active', 10)])
12           self.myImage=PhotoImage(file='c:/python33/lib/idlelib/icons/python.gif')
13           self.radioVar=IntVar()
14           Radiobutton(root, text='Radio 1', variable=self.radioVar,value=1,style='TRadiobutton',
15               command=self.ckRadioV, underline=6).grid(column=0, row=0)
16           Radiobutton(root, text='Radio 2', variable=self.radioVar,value=2,
17               style='TRadiobutton',command=self.ckRadioV).grid(column=0, row=1)
18           Radiobutton(root,text='Radio 3',variable=self.radioVar,value=3, style='TRadiobutton',
19               command=self.ckRadioV, compound=TOP,image=self.myImage).grid(column=0, row=2)
20       def ckRadioV(self):
21           temp=self.radioVar.get()
22           myLabel=Label(root,text='Radio Value: '+str(temp),width=20)
23           myLabel.grid(column=2, row=0, sticky=(E+W))
24   if __name__=="__main__":
25       root = Tk()
26       root.title("RyMax Window on the world")
27       root.geometry("300x200+200+10")#width, height, x location, y location
28       myRadio()
29       root.mainloop()
```

Text 82: RadioButton

Notebook

This is a new themed widget which allows you to be creative in organizing input and output. I have created some pretty simple 'tabs' for the sample Notebook. As you play with it notice that Ctrl Tab moves between the Notebook tabs, this is the result of us using the 'enable_traversal()' option. Type some text into the 'Start' tab and press the button. The text will show in the 'Second' Tab when you click on it. The 'Third' Tab displays the output from the Second Tab. Use the buttons on the Third Tab to hide and restore the Second

Tab. There is also an option to 'forget' a Tab, but once you click it you cannot restore the Second Tab. As this is just to show some features you will I am sure find ways to generate errors. As we are using the Text widget the cut and paste keys (Ctrl x, Ctrl V, Ctrl C)all work.

Text 83: Notebook

Notice in the final image to the right, bottom a 'blank tab' is displayed when I pressed restore after having pressed the 'forget button'.

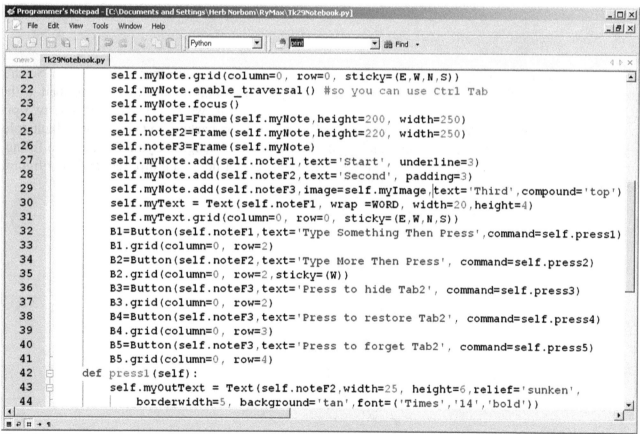

```
  1  #Python 3.3.4   Notebook                         Tk29Notebook.py
  2  from tkinter import *
  3  from tkinter.ttk import *
  4
  5  class myText():
  6      def __init__(self):
  7          myFrame=Frame(root,width=250, height=200)
  8          myFrame.grid(column=0,row=0, sticky=(E,W,N,S))
  9          self.myImage=PhotoImage(file='c:/python33/lib/idlelib/icons/python.gif')
 10          style=Style()
 11          style.theme_use('classic')
 12          style.configure("TNotebook",
 13              background='blue',
 14              foreground='white', font=('Times', '18'))
 15          style.map('TNotebook',
 16          foreground=[('active','blue')], background=[('active','green')],
 17          highlightcolor=[('focus','green'),('!focus','red')],
 18          highlightthickness=[('!active',10),('active', 10)])
 19          self.myNote= Notebook(myFrame,height=200, width=250,
 20              style='TNotebook',padding=5)   # height & width in pixels
```

Text 84: Notebook

```
 21          self.myNote.grid(column=0, row=0, sticky=(E,W,N,S))
 22          self.myNote.enable_traversal() #so you can use Ctrl Tab
 23          self.myNote.focus()
 24          self.noteF1=Frame(self.myNote,height=200, width=250)
 25          self.noteF2=Frame(self.myNote,height=220, width=250)
 26          self.noteF3=Frame(self.myNote)
 27          self.myNote.add(self.noteF1,text='Start', underline=3)
 28          self.myNote.add(self.noteF2,text='Second', padding=3)
 29          self.myNote.add(self.noteF3,image=self.myImage,text='Third',compound='top')
 30          self.myText = Text(self.noteF1, wrap =WORD, width=20,height=4)
 31          self.myText.grid(column=0, row=0, sticky=(E,W,N,S))
 32          B1=Button(self.noteF1,text='Type Something Then Press',command=self.press1)
 33          B1.grid(column=0, row=2)
 34          B2=Button(self.noteF2,text='Type More Then Press', command=self.press2)
 35          B2.grid(column=0, row=2,sticky=(W))
 36          B3=Button(self.noteF3,text='Press to hide Tab2', command=self.press3)
 37          B3.grid(column=0, row=2)
 38          B4=Button(self.noteF3,text='Press to restore Tab2', command=self.press4)
 39          B4.grid(column=0, row=3)
 40          B5=Button(self.noteF3,text='Press to forget Tab2', command=self.press5)
 41          B5.grid(column=0, row=4)
 42      def press1(self):
 43          self.myOutText = Text(self.noteF2,width=25, height=6,relief='sunken',
 44              borderwidth=5, background='tan',font=('Times','14','bold'))
```

Text 85: Notebook2

```
     Programmer's Notepad - [C:\Documents and Settings\Herb Norbom\RyMax\Tk29Notebook.py]       _ □ x
     File   Edit   View   Tools   Window   Help                                                  _ 8 x
                                         Python          ▼    print          ▼    Find  ▼
     <new>   Tk29Notebook.py                                                                     ◁ ▷ x
45          self.myOutText.grid(column=0, row=0)
46          self.myOutText.insert('1.0',self.myText.get('1.0', 'end'))
47      def press2(self):
48          myOutText = Text(self.noteF3,width=25, height=6,relief='sunken',
49              borderwidth=5, background='yellow',font=('Times','8','bold'))
50          myOutText.grid(column=0, row=0)
51          myOutText.insert('1.0',self.myOutText.get('1.0', 'end'))
52      def press3(self):
53          self.myNote.hide(self.noteF2)
54      def press4(self):
55          self.myNote.add(self.noteF2)
56      def press5(self):
57          self.myNote.forget(self.noteF2)
58
59   if __name__=="__main__":
60       root = Tk()
61       root.title("RyMax Window on the world")
62       root.geometry("275x275+200+10")#width, height, x location, y location
63       myText()
64       root.mainloop()
```

Text 86: Notebook3

Separator

The 'Separator' is a useful widget for putting a visual separation between your other widgets. The 'Separator' has only one option, set for VERTICAL or HORIZONTAL. I was able to use the columnspan with the HORIZONTAL option but I could not get the VERTICAL rowspan to work. The Separator is two pixels wide with a groove. With the 'Style' option you can only configure the background color, the default color is dark gray with a groove. You must use the 'sticky' option to stretch the length of your separator to filling the column or row. We will do a meaningless example to demonstrate. I defined a different style configuration to the vertical 'Separators'.

```
                                                                                    _ |□| ×|
 File  Edit  View  Tools  Window  Help                                               _ |❺| ×|
                         |Python      ▼|  |❡ |print|           ▼| ❊ Find  ▼|
 <new>  Tk30Separator.py *                                                          ◁ ▷ ×
   1    #Python 3.3.4 Ttk Label Examples                    Tk30Separator.py        ▲
   2    from tkinter import *
   3    from tkinter.ttk import *
   4   ⊟def separator():
   5        style=Style()    #for all buttons in program
   6        style.theme_use('classic')
   7        style.configure('TSeparator', background='red')
   8        style.configure('vertical.TSeparator', background='blue')
   9
  10        Label(root,text='nothing special').grid(column=0,row=0)
  11        Separator(root, orient=HORIZONTAL).grid(column=0, row=1,columnspan=2,sticky=(E,W))
  12        Label(root,text='more nothing special').grid(column=0,row=2)
  13   ⊟    Separator(root, orient=VERTICAL,style='vertical.TSeparator').grid(column=1,
  14            row=0,sticky=(W,N,S))
  15        Label(root,text='still more nothing special').grid(column=1,row=2)
  16   ⊟    Separator(root, orient=VERTICAL,style='vertical.TSeparator').grid(column=1,
  17            row=2,sticky=(W,N,S))
  18
  19   ⊟if __name__=="__main__":
  20        root = Tk()
  21        root.title("RyMax Window on the world")
  22        root.geometry("230x50+200+10")#width, height, x location, y location
  23        separator()
  24        root.mainloop()
```

Text 87: Separator

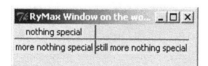

Text 88: Separator

Scrollbar

While we have been using this feature I want to go into more depth as it a themed widget. I am going to bring back our 'Text' example (Tk26Text.py) and work with just the scrollbars, Horizontal and Vertical. In our example we will be putting all the widgets on to 'root'. You would normally put them on a Frame, but just trying to keep this as straight forward as possible. I mention this because sometimes you may have more than one widget using a scrollbar and if you are not using Frames the placement can be a challenge. If you skip over the 'style and theme' for a moment you can see that you need to define a variable for each Scrollbar you are setting up. In that definition you will give instructions for what window to place the scrollbar on and its orientation. The next step is to tie your scrollbar to the widget, in our case the 'Text Widget'. You do that with the 'yscrollbarcommand or xscrollbarcommand'. The last step is to config your variable with the callback command, in our example 'barY.config(command=myText.yview)' and similar for the barX. You now have the basics for the scrollbar. We add the 'Style', 'theme' , various configure options and use the map all like we have done for other widgets. Play with the various theme's to see what you like.

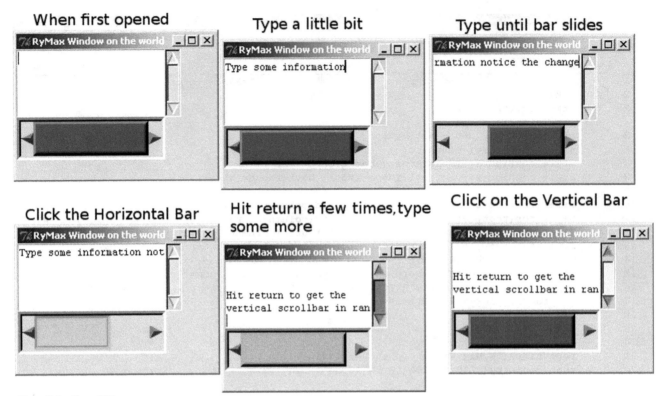

Text 89: ScrollBar

You need to set the 'wrap=None' if you want the horizontal bar to work. You can set a number of options, you may want to play with setting 'jump', repeatdelay' and 'repeatinterval' options, which are not included in these examples.

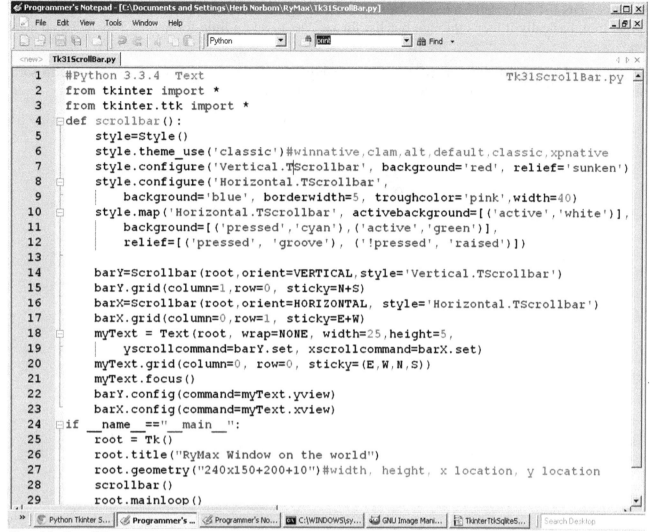

```
     1   #Python 3.3.4   Text                              Tk31ScrollBar.py
     2   from tkinter import *
     3   from tkinter.ttk import *
     4   def scrollbar():
     5       style=Style()
     6       style.theme_use('classic')#winnative,clam,alt,default,classic,xpnative
     7       style.configure('Vertical.TScrollbar', background='red', relief='sunken')
     8       style.configure('Horizontal.TScrollbar',
     9           background='blue', borderwidth=5, troughcolor='pink',width=40)
    10       style.map('Horizontal.TScrollbar', activebackground=[('active','white')],
    11           background=[('pressed','cyan'),('active','green')],
    12           relief=[('pressed', 'groove'), ('!pressed', 'raised')])
    13
    14       barY=Scrollbar(root,orient=VERTICAL,style='Vertical.TScrollbar')
    15       barY.grid(column=1,row=0, sticky=N+S)
    16       barX=Scrollbar(root,orient=HORIZONTAL, style='Horizontal.TScrollbar')
    17       barX.grid(column=0,row=1, sticky=E+W)
    18       myText = Text(root, wrap=NONE, width=25,height=5,
    19           yscrollcommand=barY.set, xscrollcommand=barX.set)
    20       myText.grid(column=0, row=0, sticky=(E,W,N,S))
    21       myText.focus()
    22       barY.config(command=myText.yview)
    23       barX.config(command=myText.xview)
    24   if __name__=="__main__":
    25       root = Tk()
    26       root.title("RyMax Window on the world")
    27       root.geometry("240x150+200+10")#width, height, x location, y location
    28       scrollbar()
    29       root.mainloop()
```

Text 90: ScrollBar

Treeview

This is a new themed widget and it adds tremendous flexibility and capability to your programs. We will start with as simple an example as we can, then we will do more examples with even greater capability.

In our first example we define three columns. Our first column will be referred to as column[0]. We can now create our Tree, which works like other widgets. We want to put our Tree in the 'root' window, our columns are equal to our previous definition and we want to show the headings. If you leave the 'show='heading' out of this program you will still get headings but you will also get the blank column. Your other option is show='tree' which will leave the heading off completely.

With our Tree defined we need to place it on the window, I continue to use grid as we have in the past.

In the next section I defined a simple list of data, just to get us going. You can of course change this around to suit you, but we are setup for three columns.

While we have defined our columns we have not defined our headings, even though it sure looked like we did. So go ahead and define the heading, and I put column width after the heading line.

At this point we have defined our Tree completely, we just need to add the data to it. We will loop through our self.tree_data list and insert each one. Note, we are using the built-in Python function "enumerate". This is a great tool, basically it loops through our list for us. Just to add a little formatting I included an 'anchor' option.

When you run the completed program you will probably say this is nice, but I want to be able to sort the columns and how about that style and theme, what about scrollbars and adding and deleting, etc.

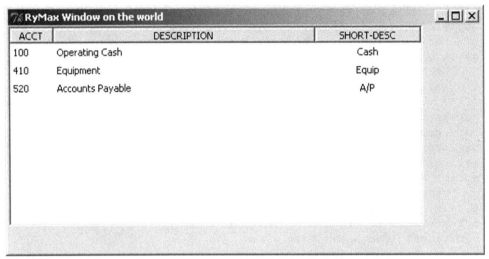

Text 91: Treeview

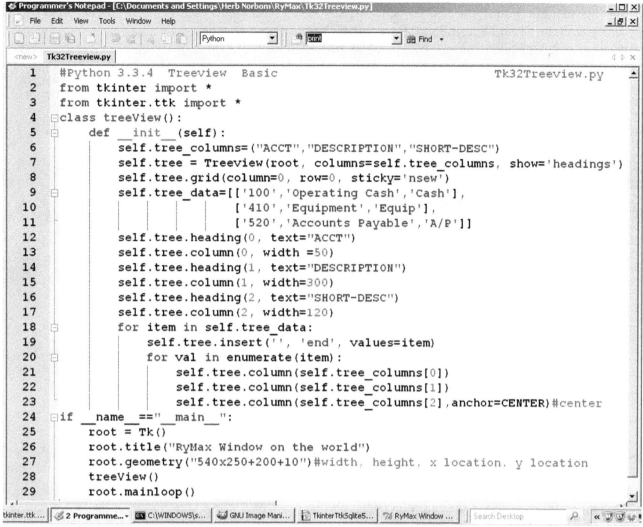

```
     1     #Python 3.3.4  Treeview  Basic                    Tk32Treeview.py
     2     from tkinter import *
     3     from tkinter.ttk import *
     4     class treeView():
     5         def __init__(self):
     6             self.tree_columns=("ACCT","DESCRIPTION","SHORT-DESC")
     7             self.tree = Treeview(root, columns=self.tree_columns, show='headings')
     8             self.tree.grid(column=0, row=0, sticky='nsew')
     9             self.tree_data=[['100','Operating Cash','Cash'],
    10                             ['410','Equipment','Equip'],
    11                             ['520','Accounts Payable','A/P']]
    12             self.tree.heading(0, text="ACCT")
    13             self.tree.column(0, width =50)
    14             self.tree.heading(1, text="DESCRIPTION")
    15             self.tree.column(1, width=300)
    16             self.tree.heading(2, text="SHORT-DESC")
    17             self.tree.column(2, width=120)
    18             for item in self.tree_data:
    19                 self.tree.insert('', 'end', values=item)
    20                 for val in enumerate(item):
    21                     self.tree.column(self.tree_columns[0])
    22                     self.tree.column(self.tree_columns[1])
    23                     self.tree.column(self.tree_columns[2],anchor=CENTER)#center
    24     if __name__=="__main__":
    25         root = Tk()
    26         root.title("RyMax Window on the world")
    27         root.geometry("540x250+200+10")#width, height, x location, y location
    28         treeView()
    29         root.mainloop()
```

Text 92: Treeview Basic

Our next Treeview program is going to add a number of features to our basic program.

Treeview using Style, Sort, Scrolling, Add and Delete

The Treeview has more features than you can shake a stick at. I have taken our basic Treeview and added quite a few features. You may notice the 'sortby' function. This is called using 'lambda', which is a function in itself that allows you to pass variables to another function. This is setup so you can sort any of the three columns just by clicking on the column heading. Within the function we use the built-in sort function. We also pass back to the originating function a setting to reverse the direction the next time the sort is called.

Because we want to use the 'Scrolling' we have placed our Tree in the 'LabelFrame, makes life a lot easier. I have defined a tuple variable to hold our column names, makes updating and referencing easier once you are used to the concept.

The vertical and horizontal scrollbars have been added. The vertical scrollbar becomes active when you have entered enough records to fill the Tree. (Copy and paste your data in the program, or use the 'Add Button' in the running program.) The horizontal scrollbar was a little more challenging for me. To make it work you will need to set a 'minwidth' for the columns. The horizontal scrollbar is not related to the data you enter in the column as you make think, but to overall column width.

To edit a row just click on it, the row contents are displayed, change to your heart's content, press 'ENTER' while you are on the Short Description field to save it to the Tree. To delete a row, select the row by clicking on it, then press the 'Delete Button'. To add a row just click on the 'Add Button', key in your data and press the 'Enter' key while on the Short Description data field.

A quick review of the 'Entry widget', we insert our data at index position '0', the data is of course our variable.

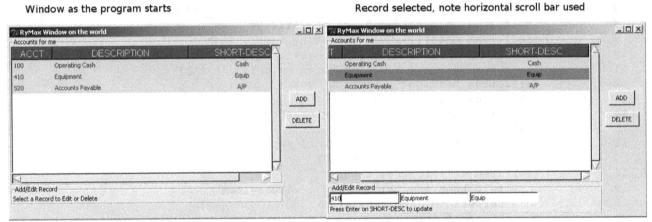

Text 93: Treeview Enhanced

As you play with this I would expect you would want to add data validation, more keys, for example the key pad Enter key just to name a couple of enhancements. My goal was to get you knee deep in the 'Tree' water with the basics. I hope you see the power of this widget. But you are probably saying, great but I want to save my data and not have it in the program or have to key it in each time. I agree, let us save our data in the Sqlite3 database. Before we take our program to the next level we need a little introduction to Sqlite3.

```python
1    #Python 3.3.4  Treeview  has Style, sort, add and delete      Tk33TreeviewBetter.py
2    from tkinter import *
3    from tkinter.ttk import *
4    def sortby(tree, column, direction):   #Sort tree contents on column heading click
5        mySortData=[(tree.set(child, column),child) #variables passed by lambda
6            for child in tree.get_children('')]
7        mySortData.sort(reverse=direction)   # reorder data
8        for indx, item in enumerate(mySortData):
9            tree.move(item[1], '', indx)
10       # switch so next time will sort in the opposite direction
11       tree.heading(column,command=lambda column=column:sortby(tree,column,
12           int(not direction))) #variables passed back by lambda
13   class treeView():
14       def __init__(self):
15           style=Style()
16           style.theme_use('classic')#winnative,clam,alt,default,classic,xpnative
17           style.configure('Treeview', background='pink', foreground='blue')
18           style.map('Treeview', background=[('selected','red')])
19           style.configure('Heading',background='blue',foreground='white',
20               font=('Times,14'))
21           myCont=Labelframe(root, text="Accounts for me",width=30)
22           myCont.grid(column=0, row=0, sticky=('nsew'))
23           self.tree_columns=("ACCT","DESCRIPTION","SHORT-DESC")
24           self.tree = Treeview(myCont, columns=self.tree_columns,
25               show='headings', style='Treeview')
26           vsb = Scrollbar(myCont,orient="vertical", command=self.tree.yview)
27           hsb = Scrollbar(myCont,orient="horizontal", command=self.tree.xview)
28           self.tree.configure(yscrollcommand=vsb.set)
29           self.tree.configure(xscrollcommand=hsb.set)
```

Text 94: Treeview Better

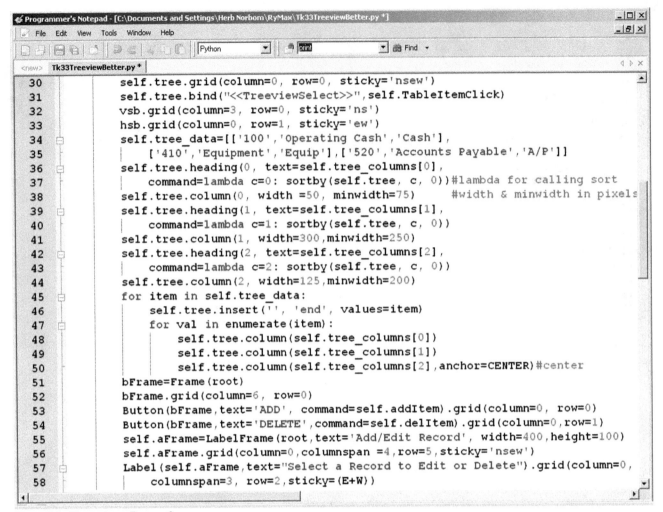

```
30          self.tree.grid(column=0, row=0, sticky='nsew')
31          self.tree.bind("<<TreeviewSelect>>",self.TableItemClick)
32          vsb.grid(column=3, row=0, sticky='ns')
33          hsb.grid(column=0, row=1, sticky='ew')
34          self.tree_data=[['100','Operating Cash','Cash'],
35              ['410','Equipment','Equip'],['520','Accounts Payable','A/P']]
36          self.tree.heading(0, text=self.tree_columns[0],
37              command=lambda c=0: sortby(self.tree, c, 0))#lambda for calling sort
38          self.tree.column(0, width =50, minwidth=75)      #width & minwidth in pixels
39          self.tree.heading(1, text=self.tree_columns[1],
40              command=lambda c=1: sortby(self.tree, c, 0))
41          self.tree.column(1, width=300,minwidth=250)
42          self.tree.heading(2, text=self.tree_columns[2],
43              command=lambda c=2: sortby(self.tree, c, 0))
44          self.tree.column(2, width=125,minwidth=200)
45          for item in self.tree_data:
46              self.tree.insert('', 'end', values=item)
47              for val in enumerate(item):
48                  self.tree.column(self.tree_columns[0])
49                  self.tree.column(self.tree_columns[1])
50                  self.tree.column(self.tree_columns[2],anchor=CENTER)#center
51          bFrame=Frame(root)
52          bFrame.grid(column=6, row=0)
53          Button(bFrame,text='ADD', command=self.addItem).grid(column=0, row=0)
54          Button(bFrame,text='DELETE',command=self.delItem).grid(column=0,row=1)
55          self.aFrame=LabelFrame(root,text='Add/Edit Record', width=400,height=100)
56          self.aFrame.grid(column=0,columnspan =4,row=5,sticky='nsew')
57          Label(self.aFrame,text="Select a Record to Edit or Delete").grid(column=0,
58              columnspan=3, row=2,sticky=(E+W))
```

Text 95: Treeview Better2

```python
59  def TableItemClick(self, event):
60      self.AddFlag=0
61      self.mySel = self.tree.focus()
62      selitems = self.tree.selection()
63      selitem= selitems[0]
64      text = self.tree.item(selitem,"value")
65      self.Acct=text[0]
66      self.Desc=text[1]
67      self.SDesc=text[2]
68      self.Entry1=Entry(self.aFrame)
69      self.Entry1.insert(0,self.Acct)
70      self.Entry1.grid(column=0,row=0)
71      self.Entry1.focus()
72      self.Entry2=Entry(self.aFrame)
73      self.Entry2.insert(0,self.Desc)
74      self.Entry2.grid(column=1,row=0)
75      self.Entry3=Entry(self.aFrame)
76      self.Entry3.insert(0,self.SDesc)
77      self.Entry3.grid(column=2,row=0)
78      self.Entry3.bind("<Return>", self.upDateAcct)
79      Label(self.aFrame,text="Press Enter on SHORT-DESC to update").grid(column=0,
80          columnspan=3, row=2,sticky=(E+W))
81  def upDateAcct(self,event):
82      if self.AddFlag==0:
83          self.tree.set(self.mySel, column='ACCT',value=self.Entry1.get())
84          self.tree.set(self.mySel, column='DESCRIPTION',value=self.Entry2.get())
85          self.tree.set(self.mySel, column='SHORT-DESC',value=self.Entry3.get())
86      if self.AddFlag==1:
87          self.tree.insert('','end',values=(self.Entry1.get(),
```

Text 96: Treeview Better3

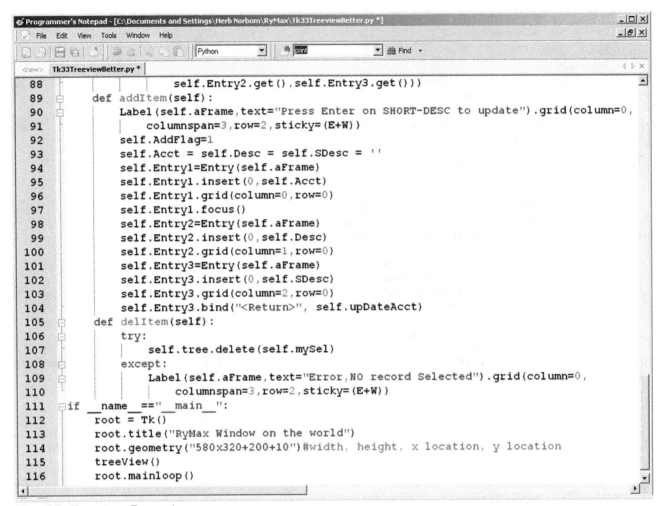

```
 88                   self.Entry2.get(),self.Entry3.get()))
 89      def addItem(self):
 90          Label(self.aFrame,text="Press Enter on SHORT-DESC to update").grid(column=0,
 91              columnspan=3,row=2,sticky=(E+W))
 92          self.AddFlag=1
 93          self.Acct = self.Desc = self.SDesc = ''
 94          self.Entry1=Entry(self.aFrame)
 95          self.Entry1.insert(0,self.Acct)
 96          self.Entry1.grid(column=0,row=0)
 97          self.Entry1.focus()
 98          self.Entry2=Entry(self.aFrame)
 99          self.Entry2.insert(0,self.Desc)
100          self.Entry2.grid(column=1,row=0)
101          self.Entry3=Entry(self.aFrame)
102          self.Entry3.insert(0,self.SDesc)
103          self.Entry3.grid(column=2,row=0)
104          self.Entry3.bind("<Return>", self.upDateAcct)
105      def delItem(self):
106          try:
107              self.tree.delete(self.mySel)
108          except:
109              Label(self.aFrame,text="Error,NO record Selected").grid(column=0,
110                  columnspan=3,row=2,sticky=(E+W))
111  if __name__=="__main__":
112      root = Tk()
113      root.title("RyMax Window on the world")
114      root.geometry("580x320+200+10")#width, height, x location, y location
115      treeView()
116      root.mainloop()
```

Text 97: Treeview Better4

Sqlite3 Introduction

Let's face it, at some point your programs need to use a database. So let's bite the bullet and go big. If you have worked with databases before the concepts should be pretty straight forward for you. If you have not don't worry we are not going to make this complicated. I am going just far enough into the concepts to get our programs to create databases and to add/edit/delete records in the database. Once you have the basic concepts down I think you will find it easier to build complexity.

As our main focus in this book is Tkinter/Ttk I am going to use that GUI as we work with Sqlite3. We are going to do several programs. The first one will simply create the database. The second one is going to be lengthy as we will add, delete and edit database records. The third one will get back to our Treeview, but with a database. (Sorry that will be lengthy also, but it will build off other programs that we have been working on.)

Simple Sqlite3 Database

In this program we will create a database 'herbDATA.db' that has two tables in it. I am not going to use Tkinter/Ttk in this program as this new topic can be confusing enough. To use a database you have to connect to it. That is the purpose of 'conn=sqlite3.connect('herbDATA.db'). In the next steps we are going to use our connection, 'conn', to execute Sqlite3 commands. To work with the database we need to designate a 'cursor', we do this with 'c=conn.cursor()'. Our first command is to drop the table if it exists. I wanted this here so you can run this program multiple times; each time the table will be deleted or dropped. Then we create the table 'chart'. The first table 'chart' will use an integer as the Primary Key, and we specify that there must be a key with the 'NOT NULL PRIMARY KEY' statement. When you create a table you need to define what it will contain and that includes the data types for each field. The data type names are not the same as we use in Python, so a short explanation is in order.

Python Data Type	Sqlite Data Type
None	NULL or null
int	INTEGER or integer
float	REAL or real
str	TEXT or text
bytes	BLOB or blob

While I am not showing 'REAL' data types in the program you need to be aware that getting exact numbers using 'REAL' can be a challenge. It comes down to the number of decimal positions to the right of the decimal point. I generally work with dollars and cents and have found it cumbersome to use 'REAL' data types. My suggestion is that you convert any float number to an integer prior to saving to your database and covert back to float if you need to when you retrieve from the database. If I want to save 50.47 to the database I do the following 'x=int(50.47 * 100)' and to convert back to float 'y=x/100'. While this may seem to be a pain if you are trying to balance two columns you will have problems if you use 'REAL' data types and have done any math on the values.

Once you have stored data in your table you will want to retrieve it. In this program we will use 'fetchall()', 'fetchone()' and 'fetchmany(size=x)'.

The second 'TABLE' in our database is name 'tranAct'. With this table I expect to have a lot of records that may be pretty much the same, so I want the database to assign the 'KEYS'. Setting up the table is pretty much the same, but here I say "ID INTEGER NOT NULL PRIMARY KEY AUTOINCREMENT". The other change is to the data that I am going to insert, notice the first data field is 'null' or 'NULL'. We need this to define a space for the KEY in non-technical terms.

I have also included an error catcher. Sqlite3 has its own exception terminology. Once you have the program running introduce an error, for example in line 33 change '-5500' to '-55A00'. You will get an 'unrecognized token: "55A00", error message. None of the insertion will occur because we have set the 'conn.rollback()' and this applies to all four of the tranAct table insertions.

You have probably noticed the lines 'conn.commit()', this saves are data in the database. While there are some procedures which automatically save your data, I recommend you use this while getting started.

After you have finished working with the database, close it with 'conn.close()'.

This has been a rapid and brief introduction, but we covered a lot of ground. I suggest you play with this program a little bit, make some changes. There is good information on line, see the Appendix for some sites that I have found to be good.

Our database is being created in the same directory as our programs. In real life you would not be doing this.

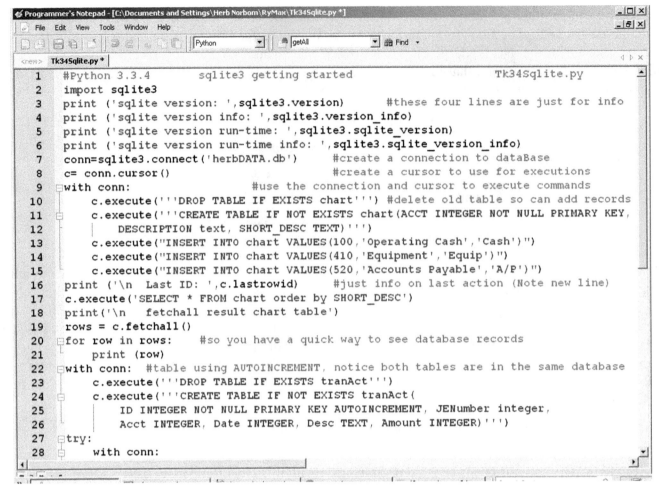

```
1    #Python 3.3.4        sqlite3 getting started              Tk34Sqlite.py
2    import sqlite3
3    print ('sqlite version: ',sqlite3.version)        #these four lines are just for info
4    print ('sqlite version info: ',sqlite3.version_info)
5    print ('sqlite version run-time: ',sqlite3.sqlite_version)
6    print ('sqlite version run-time info: ',sqlite3.sqlite_version_info)
7    conn=sqlite3.connect('herbDATA.db')        #create a connection to dataBase
8    c= conn.cursor()                           #create a cursor to use for executions
9    with conn:                     #use the connection and cursor to execute commands
10       c.execute('''DROP TABLE IF EXISTS chart''') #delete old table so can add records
11       c.execute('''CREATE TABLE IF NOT EXISTS chart(ACCT INTEGER NOT NULL PRIMARY KEY,
12           DESCRIPTION text, SHORT_DESC TEXT)''')
13       c.execute("INSERT INTO chart VALUES(100,'Operating Cash','Cash')")
14       c.execute("INSERT INTO chart VALUES(410,'Equipment','Equip')")
15       c.execute("INSERT INTO chart VALUES(520,'Accounts Payable','A/P')")
16   print ('\n  Last ID: ',c.lastrowid)       #just info on last action (Note new line)
17   c.execute('SELECT * FROM chart order by SHORT_DESC')
18   print('\n    fetchall result chart table')
19   rows = c.fetchall()
20   for row in rows:      #so you have a quick way to see database records
21       print (row)
22   with conn:  #table using AUTOINCREMENT, notice both tables are in the same database
23       c.execute('''DROP TABLE IF EXISTS tranAct''')
24       c.execute('''CREATE TABLE IF NOT EXISTS tranAct(
25           ID INTEGER NOT NULL PRIMARY KEY AUTOINCREMENT, JENumber integer,
26           Acct INTEGER, Date INTEGER, Desc TEXT, Amount INTEGER)''')
27   try:
28       with conn:
```

Text 98: Sqlite3 start

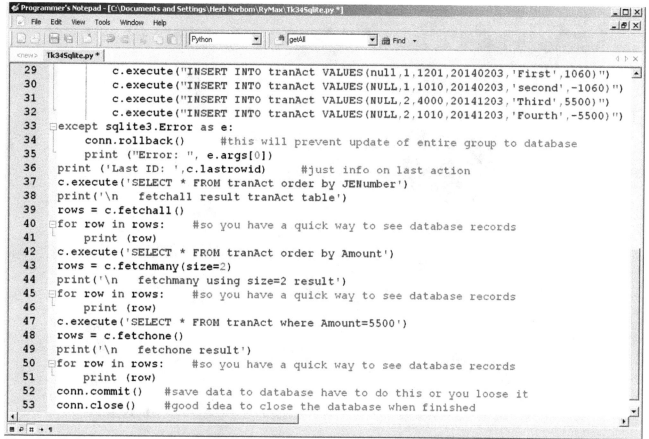

```
29        c.execute("INSERT INTO tranAct VALUES(null,1,1201,20140203,'First',1060)")
30        c.execute("INSERT INTO tranAct VALUES(NULL,1,1010,20140203,'second',-1060)")
31        c.execute("INSERT INTO tranAct VALUES(NULL,2,4000,20141203,'Third',5500)")
32        c.execute("INSERT INTO tranAct VALUES(NULL,2,1010,20141203,'Fourth',-5500)")
33  except sqlite3.Error as e:
34      conn.rollback()    #this will prevent update of entire group to database
35      print ("Error: ", e.args[0])
36  print ('Last ID: ',c.lastrowid)     #just info on last action
37  c.execute('SELECT * FROM tranAct order by JENumber')
38  print('\n   fetchall result tranAct table')
39  rows = c.fetchall()
40  for row in rows:    #so you have a quick way to see database records
41      print (row)
42  c.execute('SELECT * FROM tranAct order by Amount')
43  rows = c.fetchmany(size=2)
44  print('\n   fetchmany using size=2 result')
45  for row in rows:    #so you have a quick way to see database records
46      print (row)
47  c.execute('SELECT * FROM tranAct where Amount=5500')
48  rows = c.fetchone()
49  print('\n   fetchone result')
50  for row in rows:    #so you have a quick way to see database records
51      print (row)
52  conn.commit()    #save data to database have to do this or you loose it
53  conn.close()     #good idea to close the database when finished
```

Text 99: Sqlite3 start2

The following gives you an idea of the output that we printed to the console.

```
C:\WINDOWS\system32\cmd.exe                               _ |□| X

C:\Documents and Settings\Herb Norbom\RyMax>python tk34sqlite.py
sqlite version:  2.6.0
sqlite version info:  (2, 6, 0)
sqlite version run-time:  3.7.12
sqlite version run-time info:  (3, 7, 12)

   Last ID:  520

     fetchall result chart table
(520, 'Accounts Payable', 'A/P')
(100, 'Operating Cash', 'Cash')
(410, 'Equipment', 'Equip')
Last ID:  4

     fetchall result tranAct table
(1, 1, 1201, 20140203, 'First', 1060)
(2, 1, 1010, 20140203, 'second', -1060)
(3, 2, 4000, 20141203, 'Third', 5500)
(4, 2, 1010, 20141203, 'Fourth', -5500)

     fetchmany using size=2 result
(4, 2, 1010, 20141203, 'Fourth', -5500)
(2, 1, 1010, 20140203, 'second', -1060)

     fetchone result
3
2
4000
20141203
Third
5500
```

Text 100: sqlite3 start Result

Sqlite3 Query, Add, Edit, Delete using Tkinter/Ttk

Our next program gets a little leggy, but it does do a lot. I don't consider this code to be the 'best', but one of my goals is to keep the code as readable as I can. So I hope you can put up with my style and take the ideas and write your code using your style. The other thing I want to explain is that my examples are not intended to catch all errors, they should, I hope, keep running, but it the real world you would have a lot of code in place for keeping your users in line and your data safe.

With that said on to our next program. This will get you a little familiar with using your database with Tkinter/Ttk. I am not going to use the style/theme features as the program is long enough without that. This program builds on the knowledge we have collected to date. I think there are only a couple of totally new items. 'UPDATING, DELETING' database records. One other new item is where we get a rowcount. Sqlite3 will return a '1' if your last action was successful and a '0' if not. Also, you will see an ending comma "," where I define what record to select from the database, it is required.

After you have the program running and want to clean up your data base you can run our previous program to recreate the database. If you just delete the database this current program will not work as it is not setup to create the tables.

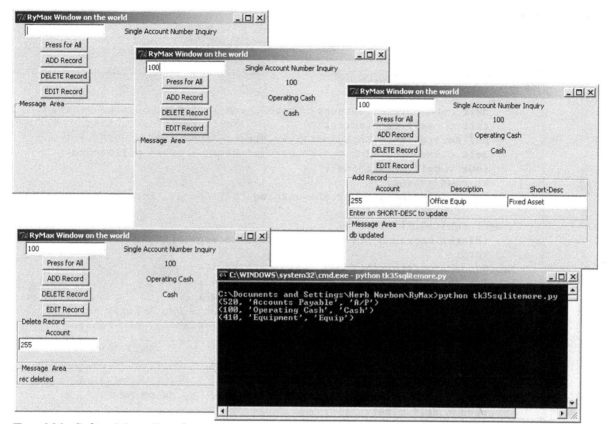

Text 101: Sqlite More Result

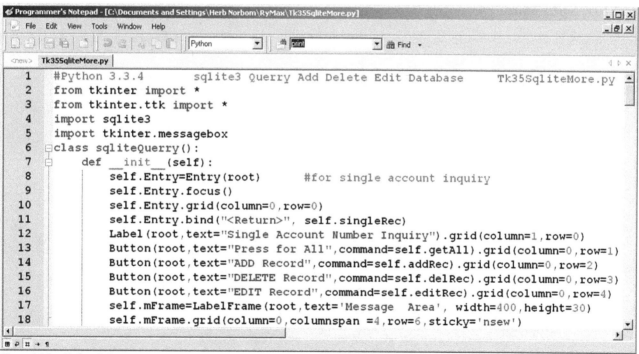

```
1    #Python 3.3.4        sqlite3 Querry Add Delete Edit Database      Tk35SqliteMore.py
2    from tkinter import *
3    from tkinter.ttk import *
4    import sqlite3
5    import tkinter.messagebox
6    class sqliteQuerry():
7        def __init__(self):
8            self.Entry=Entry(root)        #for single account inquiry
9            self.Entry.focus()
10           self.Entry.grid(column=0,row=0)
11           self.Entry.bind("<Return>", self.singleRec)
12           Label(root,text="Single Account Number Inquiry").grid(column=1,row=0)
13           Button(root,text="Press for All",command=self.getAll).grid(column=0,row=1)
14           Button(root,text="ADD Record",command=self.addRec).grid(column=0,row=2)
15           Button(root,text="DELETE Record",command=self.delRec).grid(column=0,row=3)
16           Button(root,text="EDIT Record",command=self.editRec).grid(column=0,row=4)
17           self.mFrame=LabelFrame(root,text='Message  Area', width=400,height=30)
18           self.mFrame.grid(column=0,columnspan =4,row=6,sticky='nsew')
```

Text 102: SqliteMore

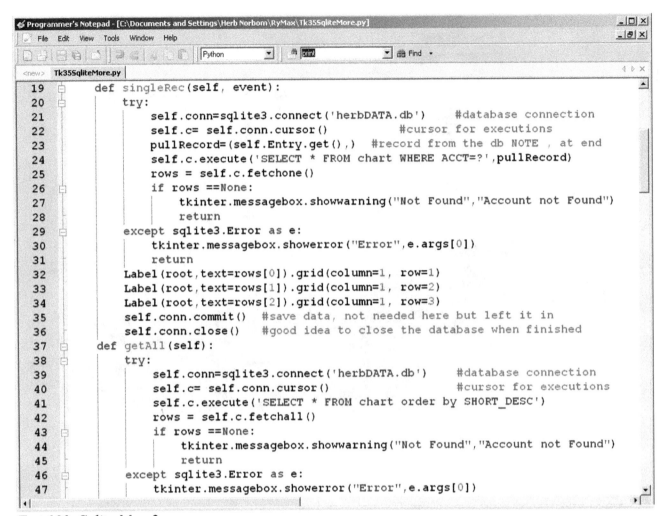

```
 19    def singleRec(self, event):
 20        try:
 21            self.conn=sqlite3.connect('herbDATA.db')    #database connection
 22            self.c= self.conn.cursor()         #cursor for executions
 23            pullRecord=(self.Entry.get(),)  #record from the db NOTE , at end
 24            self.c.execute('SELECT * FROM chart WHERE ACCT=?',pullRecord)
 25            rows = self.c.fetchone()
 26            if rows ==None:
 27                tkinter.messagebox.showwarning("Not Found","Account not Found")
 28                return
 29        except sqlite3.Error as e:
 30            tkinter.messagebox.showerror("Error",e.args[0])
 31            return
 32        Label(root,text=rows[0]).grid(column=1, row=1)
 33        Label(root,text=rows[1]).grid(column=1, row=2)
 34        Label(root,text=rows[2]).grid(column=1, row=3)
 35        self.conn.commit()  #save data, not needed here but left it in
 36        self.conn.close()    #good idea to close the database when finished
 37    def getAll(self):
 38        try:
 39            self.conn=sqlite3.connect('herbDATA.db')       #database connection
 40            self.c= self.conn.cursor()                  #cursor for executions
 41            self.c.execute('SELECT * FROM chart order by SHORT_DESC')
 42            rows = self.c.fetchall()
 43            if rows ==None:
 44                tkinter.messagebox.showwarning("Not Found","Account not Found")
 45                return
 46        except sqlite3.Error as e:
 47            tkinter.messagebox.showerror("Error",e.args[0])
```

Text 103: Sqlite More2

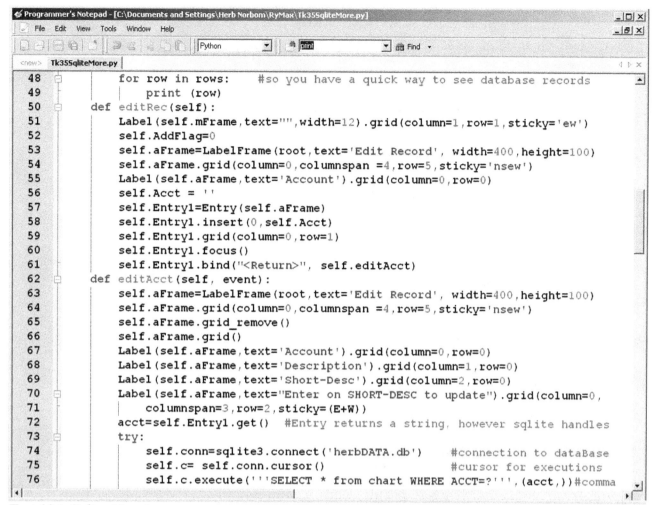

```
48          for row in rows:       #so you have a quick way to see database records
49              print (row)
50      def editRec(self):
51          Label(self.mFrame,text="",width=12).grid(column=1,row=1,sticky='ew')
52          self.AddFlag=0
53          self.aFrame=LabelFrame(root,text='Edit Record', width=400,height=100)
54          self.aFrame.grid(column=0,columnspan =4,row=5,sticky='nsew')
55          Label(self.aFrame,text='Account').grid(column=0,row=0)
56          self.Acct = ''
57          self.Entry1=Entry(self.aFrame)
58          self.Entry1.insert(0,self.Acct)
59          self.Entry1.grid(column=0,row=1)
60          self.Entry1.focus()
61          self.Entry1.bind("<Return>", self.editAcct)
62      def editAcct(self, event):
63          self.aFrame=LabelFrame(root,text='Edit Record', width=400,height=100)
64          self.aFrame.grid(column=0,columnspan =4,row=5,sticky='nsew')
65          self.aFrame.grid_remove()
66          self.aFrame.grid()
67          Label(self.aFrame,text='Account').grid(column=0,row=0)
68          Label(self.aFrame,text='Description').grid(column=1,row=0)
69          Label(self.aFrame,text='Short-Desc').grid(column=2,row=0)
70          Label(self.aFrame,text="Enter on SHORT-DESC to update").grid(column=0,
71              columnspan=3,row=2,sticky=(E+W))
72          acct=self.Entry1.get()  #Entry returns a string, however sqlite handles
73          try:
74              self.conn=sqlite3.connect('herbDATA.db')     #connection to dataBase
75              self.c= self.conn.cursor()                   #cursor for executions
76              self.c.execute('''SELECT * from chart WHERE ACCT=?''',(acct,))#comma
```

Text 104: Sqlite More3

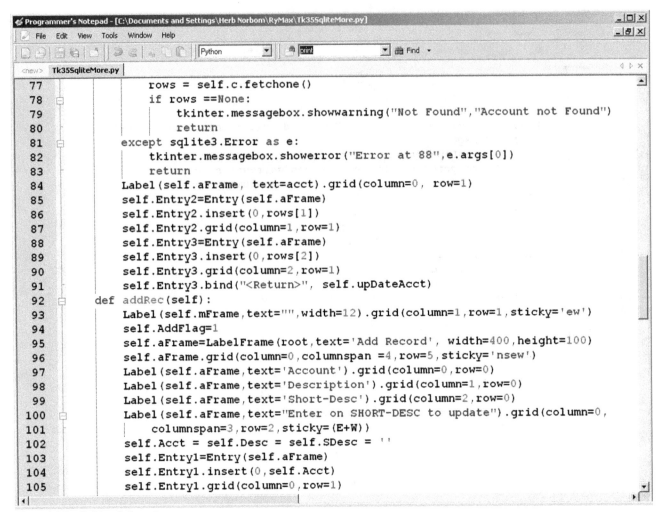

```
77          rows = self.c.fetchone()
78          if rows ==None:
79              tkinter.messagebox.showwarning("Not Found","Account not Found")
80              return
81      except sqlite3.Error as e:
82          tkinter.messagebox.showerror("Error at 88",e.args[0])
83          return
84      Label(self.aFrame, text=acct).grid(column=0, row=1)
85      self.Entry2=Entry(self.aFrame)
86      self.Entry2.insert(0,rows[1])
87      self.Entry2.grid(column=1,row=1)
88      self.Entry3=Entry(self.aFrame)
89      self.Entry3.insert(0,rows[2])
90      self.Entry3.grid(column=2,row=1)
91      self.Entry3.bind("<Return>", self.upDateAcct)
92  def addRec(self):
93      Label(self.mFrame,text="",width=12).grid(column=1,row=1,sticky='ew')
94      self.AddFlag=1
95      self.aFrame=LabelFrame(root,text='Add Record', width=400,height=100)
96      self.aFrame.grid(column=0,columnspan =4,row=5,sticky='nsew')
97      Label(self.aFrame,text='Account').grid(column=0,row=0)
98      Label(self.aFrame,text='Description').grid(column=1,row=0)
99      Label(self.aFrame,text='Short-Desc').grid(column=2,row=0)
100     Label(self.aFrame,text="Enter on SHORT-DESC to update").grid(column=0,
101         columnspan=3,row=2,sticky=(E+W))
102     self.Acct = self.Desc = self.SDesc = ''
103     self.Entry1=Entry(self.aFrame)
104     self.Entry1.insert(0,self.Acct)
105     self.Entry1.grid(column=0,row=1)
```

Text 105: Sqlite More4

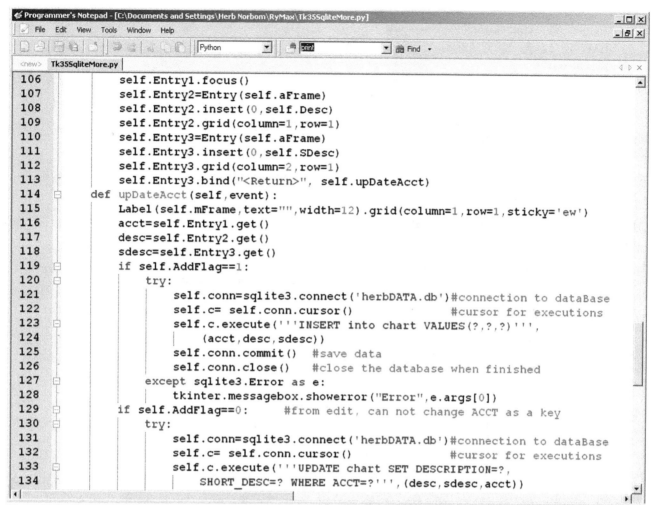

```
106          self.Entry1.focus()
107          self.Entry2=Entry(self.aFrame)
108          self.Entry2.insert(0,self.Desc)
109          self.Entry2.grid(column=1,row=1)
110          self.Entry3=Entry(self.aFrame)
111          self.Entry3.insert(0,self.SDesc)
112          self.Entry3.grid(column=2,row=1)
113          self.Entry3.bind("<Return>", self.upDateAcct)
114      def upDateAcct(self,event):
115          Label(self.mFrame,text="",width=12).grid(column=1,row=1,sticky='ew')
116          acct=self.Entry1.get()
117          desc=self.Entry2.get()
118          sdesc=self.Entry3.get()
119          if self.AddFlag==1:
120              try:
121                  self.conn=sqlite3.connect('herbDATA.db')#connection to dataBase
122                  self.c= self.conn.cursor()                #cursor for executions
123                  self.c.execute('''INSERT into chart VALUES(?,?,?)''',
124                      (acct,desc,sdesc))
125                  self.conn.commit() #save data
126                  self.conn.close()   #close the database when finished
127              except sqlite3.Error as e:
128                  tkinter.messagebox.showerror("Error",e.args[0])
129          if self.AddFlag==0:      #from edit, can not change ACCT as a key
130              try:
131                  self.conn=sqlite3.connect('herbDATA.db')#connection to dataBase
132                  self.c= self.conn.cursor()                #cursor for executions
133                  self.c.execute('''UPDATE chart SET DESCRIPTION=?,
134                      SHORT_DESC=? WHERE ACCT=?''',(desc,sdesc,acct))
```

Text 106: Sqlite More5

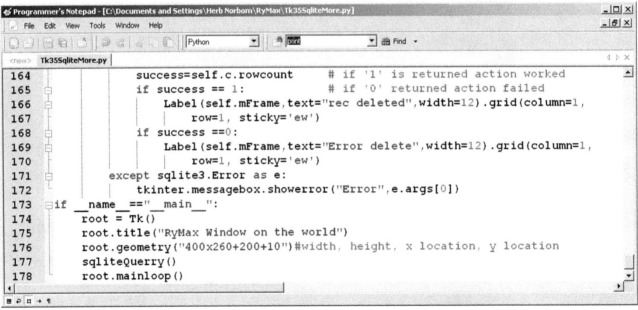

```python
                    self.conn.commit()    #save data
                    self.conn.close()     #close the database when finished
                except sqlite3.Error as e:
                    tkinter.messagebox.showerror("Error",e.args[0])
            success=self.c.rowcount       # if '1' is returned action worked
            if success == 1:              # if '0' returned action failed
                Label(self.mFrame,text="db updated",width=12).grid(column=1,
                    row=1,sticky='ew')
            if success ==0:
                Label(self.mFrame,text="db Error",width=12).grid(column=1,
                    row=1,sticky='ew')
    def delRec(self):
        self.aFrame=LabelFrame(root,text='Delete Record', width=400,height=100)
        self.aFrame.grid(column=0,columnspan =4,row=5,sticky='nsew')
        Label(self.aFrame,text='Account').grid(column=0,row=0)
        self.Acct = ''
        self.Entry1=Entry(self.aFrame)
        self.Entry1.insert(0,self.Acct)
        self.Entry1.grid(column=0,row=1)
        self.Entry1.focus()
        self.Entry1.bind("<Return>", self.deleteAcct)
    def deleteAcct(self,event):
        acct=self.Entry1.get()
        try:
            self.conn=sqlite3.connect('herbDATA.db')       #connection to dataBase
            self.c= self.conn.cursor()                     #cursor for executions
            self.c.execute('''DELETE from chart WHERE ACCT=?''',(acct,))
            self.conn.commit()  #save data
            self.conn.close()   #good idea to close the database when finished
```

Text 107: Sqlite More 6

```python
            success=self.c.rowcount       # if '1' is returned action worked
            if success == 1:              # if '0' returned action failed
                Label(self.mFrame,text="rec deleted",width=12).grid(column=1,
                    row=1, sticky='ew')
            if success ==0:
                Label(self.mFrame,text="Error delete",width=12).grid(column=1,
                    row=1, sticky='ew')
        except sqlite3.Error as e:
            tkinter.messagebox.showerror("Error",e.args[0])
if __name__=="__main__":
    root = Tk()
    root.title("RyMax Window on the world")
    root.geometry("400x260+200+10")#width, height, x location, y location
    sqliteQuerry()
    root.mainloop()
```

Text 108: Sqlite More7

Sqlite with Treeview

From that roundabout way we have arrived at our end goal of marrying Sqlite3 with Tkinter/Ttk Treeview. This as I am sure you have guessed is a fairly long program. The good news is that I will use Tk33TreeviewBetter.py as the base program and add to it what we need for Sqlite3. Where I would delete code lines I have just commented them out, so you can easily identify them. For new code, if a single line, I put a '#NEW' comment at the end of the line. Where there is a block of new code, I have put a comment on the Left Margin indicating start and end positions.

I am going to set flags for what action I want to do on the database, insert, delete or update. This allows me to have one section of the program for working with Sqlite. I do however need to setup the initial read of the database and loading of the database records into Treeview. As you play with the program I am sure you will find it could use some tweaking, but after all this is just a demo. I have run Tk34Sqlite.py to reset or create the database.

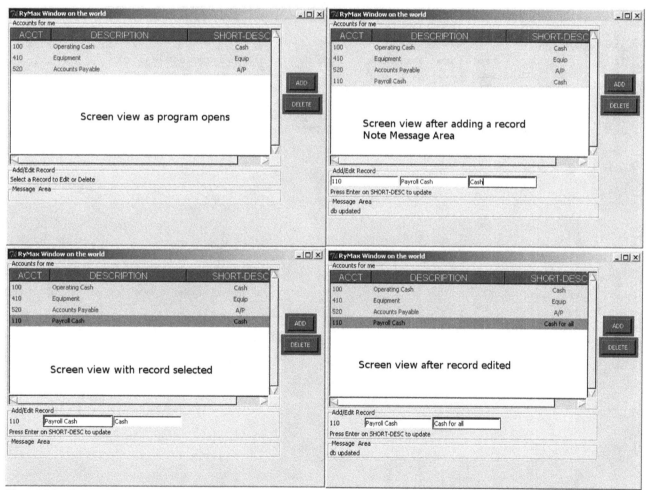

Text 109: Sqlite Treeview

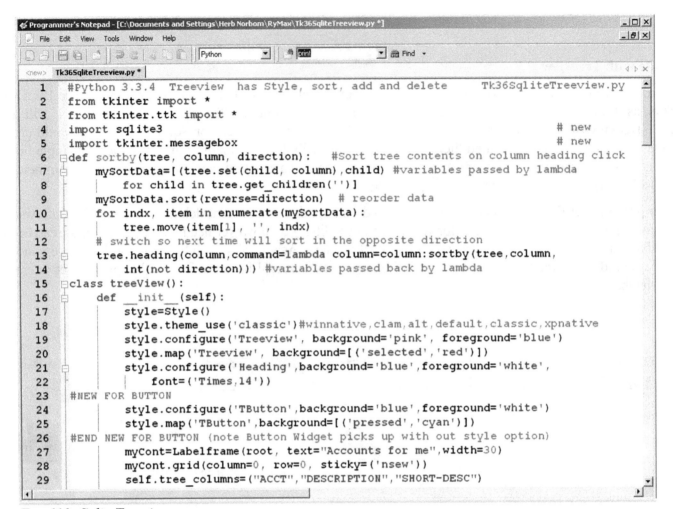

```python
#Python 3.3.4  Treeview  has Style, sort, add and delete       Tk36SqliteTreeview.py
from tkinter import *
from tkinter.ttk import *
import sqlite3                                              # new
import tkinter.messagebox                                  # new
def sortby(tree, column, direction):   #Sort tree contents on column heading click
    mySortData=[(tree.set(child, column),child) #variables passed by lambda
        for child in tree.get_children('')]
    mySortData.sort(reverse=direction)   # reorder data
    for indx, item in enumerate(mySortData):
        tree.move(item[1], '', indx)
    # switch so next time will sort in the opposite direction
    tree.heading(column,command=lambda column=column:sortby(tree,column,
        int(not direction))) #variables passed back by lambda
class treeView():
    def __init__(self):
        style=Style()
        style.theme_use('classic')#winnative,clam,alt,default,classic,xpnative
        style.configure('Treeview', background='pink', foreground='blue')
        style.map('Treeview', background=[('selected','red')])
        style.configure('Heading',background='blue',foreground='white',
            font=('Times,14'))
#NEW FOR BUTTON
        style.configure('TButton',background='blue',foreground='white')
        style.map('TButton',background=[('pressed','cyan')])
#END NEW FOR BUTTON (note Button Widget picks up with out style option)
        myCont=Labelframe(root, text="Accounts for me",width=30)
        myCont.grid(column=0, row=0, sticky=('nsew'))
        self.tree_columns=("ACCT","DESCRIPTION","SHORT-DESC")
```

Text 110: SqliteTreeview

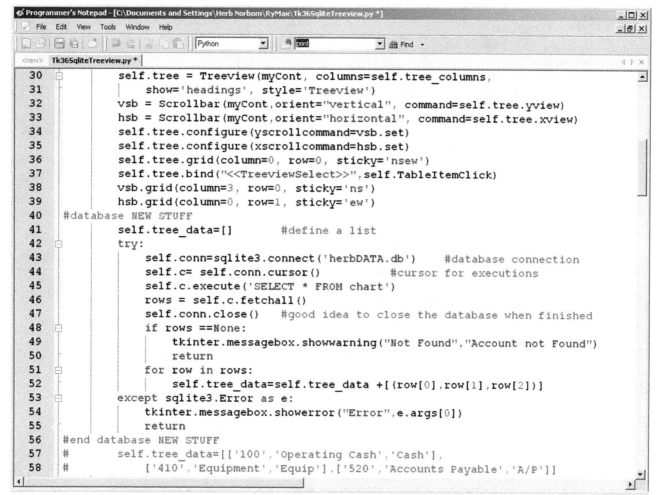

```
30      self.tree = Treeview(myCont, columns=self.tree_columns,
31          show='headings', style='Treeview')
32      vsb = Scrollbar(myCont,orient="vertical", command=self.tree.yview)
33      hsb = Scrollbar(myCont,orient="horizontal", command=self.tree.xview)
34      self.tree.configure(yscrollcommand=vsb.set)
35      self.tree.configure(xscrollcommand=hsb.set)
36      self.tree.grid(column=0, row=0, sticky='nsew')
37      self.tree.bind("<<TreeviewSelect>>",self.TableItemClick)
38      vsb.grid(column=3, row=0, sticky='ns')
39      hsb.grid(column=0, row=1, sticky='ew')
40  #database NEW STUFF
41      self.tree_data=[]        #define a list
42      try:
43          self.conn=sqlite3.connect('herbDATA.db')    #database connection
44          self.c= self.conn.cursor()           #cursor for executions
45          self.c.execute('SELECT * FROM chart')
46          rows = self.c.fetchall()
47          self.conn.close()   #good idea to close the database when finished
48          if rows ==None:
49              tkinter.messagebox.showwarning("Not Found","Account not Found")
50              return
51          for row in rows:
52              self.tree_data=self.tree_data +[(row[0],row[1],row[2])]
53      except sqlite3.Error as e:
54          tkinter.messagebox.showerror("Error",e.args[0])
55          return
56  #end database NEW STUFF
57  #      self.tree_data=[['100','Operating Cash','Cash'],
58  #          ['410','Equipment','Equip'],['520','Accounts Payable','A/P']]
```

Text 111: SqliteTreeview2

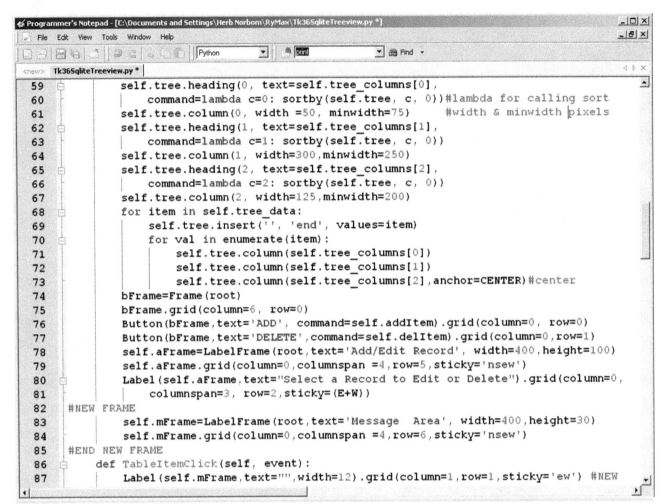

```
59    self.tree.heading(0, text=self.tree_columns[0],
60        command=lambda c=0: sortby(self.tree, c, 0))#lambda for calling sort
61    self.tree.column(0, width =50, minwidth=75)      #width & minwidth pixels
62    self.tree.heading(1, text=self.tree_columns[1],
63        command=lambda c=1: sortby(self.tree, c, 0))
64    self.tree.column(1, width=300,minwidth=250)
65    self.tree.heading(2, text=self.tree_columns[2],
66        command=lambda c=2: sortby(self.tree, c, 0))
67    self.tree.column(2, width=125,minwidth=200)
68    for item in self.tree_data:
69        self.tree.insert('', 'end', values=item)
70        for val in enumerate(item):
71            self.tree.column(self.tree_columns[0])
72            self.tree.column(self.tree_columns[1])
73            self.tree.column(self.tree_columns[2],anchor=CENTER)#center
74    bFrame=Frame(root)
75    bFrame.grid(column=6, row=0)
76    Button(bFrame,text='ADD', command=self.addItem).grid(column=0, row=0)
77    Button(bFrame,text='DELETE',command=self.delItem).grid(column=0,row=1)
78    self.aFrame=LabelFrame(root,text='Add/Edit Record', width=400,height=100)
79    self.aFrame.grid(column=0,columnspan =4,row=5,sticky='nsew')
80    Label(self.aFrame,text="Select a Record to Edit or Delete").grid(column=0,
81        columnspan=3, row=2,sticky=(E+W))
82 #NEW FRAME
83    self.mFrame=LabelFrame(root,text='Message  Area', width=400,height=30)
84    self.mFrame.grid(column=0,columnspan =4,row=6,sticky='nsew')
85 #END NEW FRAME
86    def TableItemClick(self, event):
87        Label(self.mFrame,text="",width=12).grid(column=1,row=1,sticky='ew') #NEW
```

Text 112: SqliteTreeview3

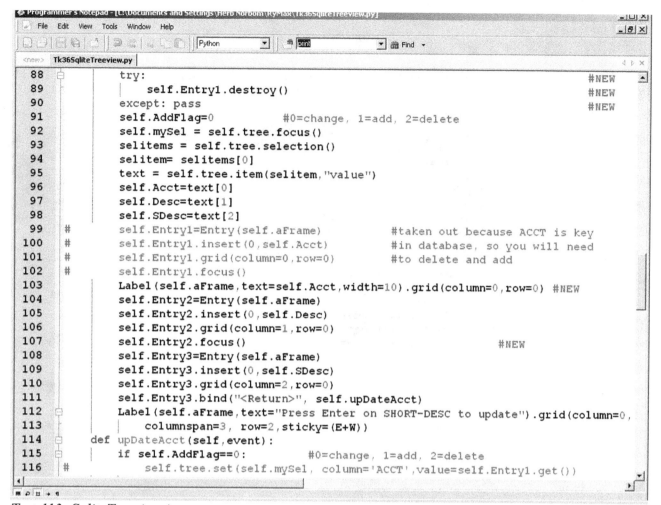

```
88        try:                                                    #NEW
89            self.Entry1.destroy()                               #NEW
90        except: pass                                            #NEW
91        self.AddFlag=0              #0=change, 1=add, 2=delete
92        self.mySel = self.tree.focus()
93        selitems = self.tree.selection()
94        selitem= selitems[0]
95        text = self.tree.item(selitem,"value")
96        self.Acct=text[0]
97        self.Desc=text[1]
98        self.SDesc=text[2]
99    #   self.Entry1=Entry(self.aFrame)          #taken out because ACCT is key
100   #   self.Entry1.insert(0,self.Acct)         #in database, so you will need
101   #   self.Entry1.grid(column=0,row=0)        #to delete and add
102   #   self.Entry1.focus()
103       Label(self.aFrame,text=self.Acct,width=10).grid(column=0,row=0) #NEW
104       self.Entry2=Entry(self.aFrame)
105       self.Entry2.insert(0,self.Desc)
106       self.Entry2.grid(column=1,row=0)
107       self.Entry2.focus()                                    #NEW
108       self.Entry3=Entry(self.aFrame)
109       self.Entry3.insert(0,self.SDesc)
110       self.Entry3.grid(column=2,row=0)
111       self.Entry3.bind("<Return>", self.upDateAcct)
112       Label(self.aFrame,text="Press Enter on SHORT-DESC to update").grid(column=0,
113           columnspan=3, row=2,sticky=(E+W))
114   def upDateAcct(self,event):
115       if self.AddFlag==0:              #0=change, 1=add, 2=delete
116   #       self.tree.set(self.mySel, column='ACCT',value=self.Entry1.get())
```

Text 113: SqliteTreeview4

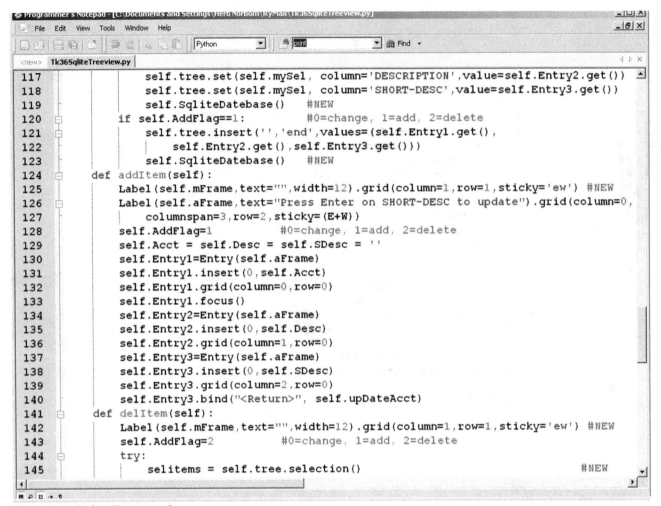

```
117          self.tree.set(self.mySel, column='DESCRIPTION',value=self.Entry2.get())
118          self.tree.set(self.mySel, column='SHORT-DESC',value=self.Entry3.get())
119          self.SqliteDatebase()     #NEW
120      if self.AddFlag==1:          #0=change, 1=add, 2=delete
121          self.tree.insert('','end',values=(self.Entry1.get(),
122              self.Entry2.get(),self.Entry3.get()))
123          self.SqliteDatebase()     #NEW
124  def addItem(self):
125      Label(self.mFrame,text="",width=12).grid(column=1,row=1,sticky='ew') #NEW
126      Label(self.aFrame,text="Press Enter on SHORT-DESC to update").grid(column=0,
127          columnspan=3,row=2,sticky=(E+W))
128      self.AddFlag=1           #0=change, 1=add, 2=delete
129      self.Acct = self.Desc = self.SDesc = ''
130      self.Entry1=Entry(self.aFrame)
131      self.Entry1.insert(0,self.Acct)
132      self.Entry1.grid(column=0,row=0)
133      self.Entry1.focus()
134      self.Entry2=Entry(self.aFrame)
135      self.Entry2.insert(0,self.Desc)
136      self.Entry2.grid(column=1,row=0)
137      self.Entry3=Entry(self.aFrame)
138      self.Entry3.insert(0,self.SDesc)
139      self.Entry3.grid(column=2,row=0)
140      self.Entry3.bind("<Return>", self.upDateAcct)
141  def delItem(self):
142      Label(self.mFrame,text="",width=12).grid(column=1,row=1,sticky='ew') #NEW
143      self.AddFlag=2           #0=change, 1=add, 2=delete
144      try:
145          selitems = self.tree.selection()                      #NEW
```

Text 114: SqliteTreeview5

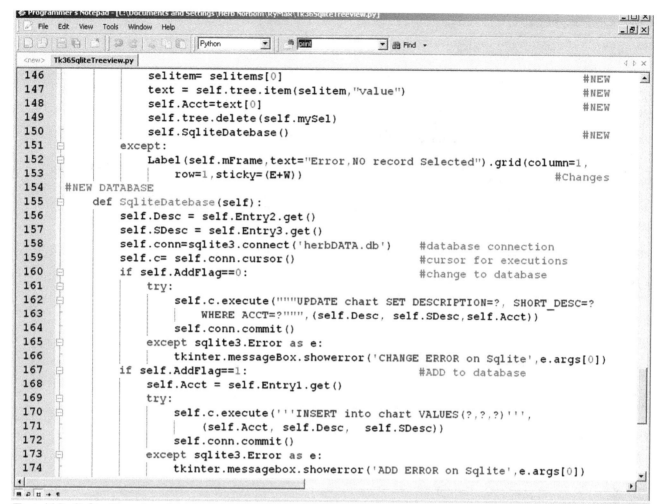

```
146              selitem= selitems[0]                              #NEW
147              text = self.tree.item(selitem,"value")            #NEW
148              self.Acct=text[0]                                 #NEW
149              self.tree.delete(self.mySel)
150              self.SqliteDatebase()                             #NEW
151          except:
152              Label(self.mFrame,text="Error,NO record Selected").grid(column=1,
153                  row=1,sticky=(E+W))                           #Changes
154  #NEW DATABASE
155      def SqliteDatebase(self):
156          self.Desc = self.Entry2.get()
157          self.SDesc = self.Entry3.get()
158          self.conn=sqlite3.connect('herbDATA.db')      #database connection
159          self.c= self.conn.cursor()                    #cursor for executions
160          if self.AddFlag==0:                           #change to database
161              try:
162                  self.c.execute("""UPDATE chart SET DESCRIPTION=?, SHORT_DESC=?
163                      WHERE ACCT=?""",(self.Desc, self.SDesc,self.Acct))
164                  self.conn.commit()
165              except sqlite3.Error as e:
166                  tkinter.messageBox.showerror('CHANGE ERROR on Sqlite',e.args[0])
167          if self.AddFlag==1:                           #ADD to database
168              self.Acct = self.Entry1.get()
169              try:
170                  self.c.execute('''INSERT into chart VALUES(?,?,?)''',
171                      (self.Acct, self.Desc,  self.SDesc))
172                  self.conn.commit()
173              except sqlite3.Error as e:
174                  tkinter.messagebox.showerror('ADD ERROR on Sqlite',e.args[0])
```

Text 115: SqliteTreeview6

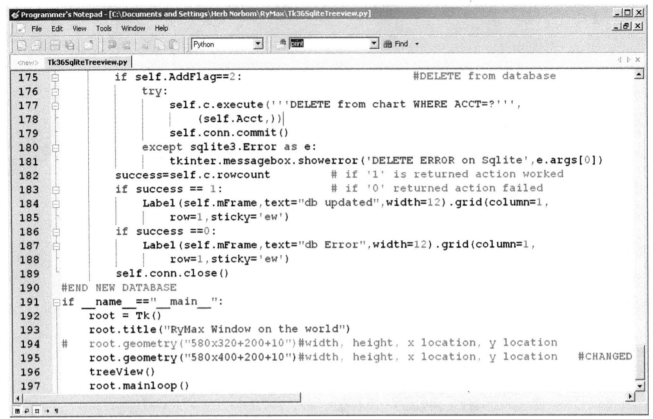

```
175          if self.AddFlag==2:                    #DELETE from database
176              try:
177                  self.c.execute('''DELETE from chart WHERE ACCT=?''',
178                      (self.Acct,))|
179                  self.conn.commit()
180              except sqlite3.Error as e:
181                  tkinter.messagebox.showerror('DELETE ERROR on Sqlite',e.args[0])
182          success=self.c.rowcount        # if '1' is returned action worked
183          if success == 1:               # if '0' returned action failed
184              Label(self.mFrame,text="db updated",width=12).grid(column=1,
185                  row=1,sticky='ew')
186          if success ==0:
187              Label(self.mFrame,text="db Error",width=12).grid(column=1,
188                  row=1,sticky='ew')
189          self.conn.close()
190  #END NEW DATABASE
191  if __name__=="__main__":
192      root = Tk()
193      root.title("RyMax Window on the world")
194  #    root.geometry("580x320+200+10")#width, height, x location, y location
195      root.geometry("580x400+200+10")#width, height, x location, y location    #CHANGED
196      treeView()
197      root.mainloop()
```

Text 116: SqliteTreeView7

THE END OR THE BEGINNING

I hope that you have learned a lot and had some fun. If you created the programs I hope you keep them and find them as well as the book to be good reference tools. These programs can be a good start to building your code library. Visit the web site www.rymax.biz for additional information. I would like to learn from your experience, you can e-mail me at herb@rymax.biz.

APPENDIX

Where to get Python

- www.activestate.com   The Community Edition as it is FREE. This is a great site, I suggest you go ahead and register on it. As you will see later, they have some great tools for downloading other modules that you may need.

- www.sourceforge.net is also a great site and it is a good idea to register here also. You can do searches for software modules. This site also has great download tools.

I like the ActiveState® site because it is very user friendly. I have found it easy to use for adding Python modules. A general hint, unless you have a great memory and know what you are doing, use the defaults when installing programs.

Programmer's Notepad

Go to http://winavr.sourceforge.net/download.html.   Select download and follow the instructions. The version we are using here is WinAvr-2010 and is approximately 28.8Mb. The editor is called Programmer's Notepad.

Geany

For Windows go to http://www.geany.org/ . The geany-1.2.3.1 setup.exe Full Installer is approximately 8Mb. For Linux, pretty straight forward, you can use 'sudo apt-get install geany.

Hardware and Operating Systems used

Windows

Microsoft Windows XP Professional Version 2002. Service Pack 3 on a Dell Dimension PC with Pentium4 CPU 3.00GHz.

Linux

Debian Release 7.6 (wheezy) 32-bit. On an old PC with an Intel(R) Pentium(R) 4 CPU 2.40GHz. The Kernel Linux is 3.2.0 -4-686. I am using the Xfce Desktop Environment, Version 4.8. I also have the GNOME Desktop 3.4.2 installed. I am using the bash shell. Programs are run under Active Python 3.3.4.1. Special note images locations shown in program are not the same for Linux, edit as appropriate. In my case the image files were in the following locations:

myImage=PhotoImage(file='/opt/ActivePython-3.3/lib/python3.3/idlelib/Icons/python.gif')
myImage=PhotoImage(file='/opt/ActivePython-3.3/lib/tk8.5/demos/images/earth.gif')
myBitMap = BitmapImage(file='/opt/ActivePython-3.3/lib/tk8.5/demos/images/face.xbm')

Window sizes may need to be adjusted.

The shell script I am using is shown in the following. Execute with a "." and a space before the filename, for example ". searchPath". Depending on your system setup you may need to make it executable.

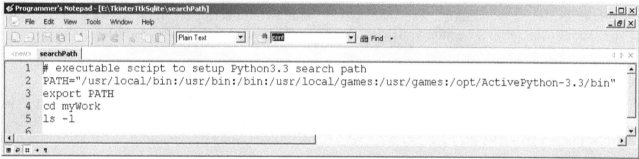

Text 117: Linux Script for Python Path

To run program from command prompt   'python3 Tk1Button.py' for example.

Raspberry Pi

The Raspberry Pi is running Linux Raspbian, Kernel 3.12.22 #691, version wheezy. The Debian-Linux version is 7.6. Python 3.2.3 software is used. The images I used in the examples were located in:

/usr/share/doc/tk8.5/examples/images/earth.gif
/usr/lib/python3.2/idlelib/Icons/python.gif

With my version of Python I did not need to set a path. To run program from command prompt 'python3 Tk1Button.py' for example.

Windows Command Line

There are a number of ways to get to the Windows command line. Depending on your Windows version of the following should work.

• On Start Menu, click on the "Run" button. Enter 'cmd'. This will open a DOS window in your default director. This director is a good place to have your reference library of programs that we will create.

- Press the Windows Key and the 'r' key simultaneously The 'Run" window opens, enter 'cmd', then same as above.

Simple DOS commands

Before we go any further, a few quick words on DOS commands. They can do damage, they are not very user friendly; they will destroy without asking twice. So make sure the command you enter is the command that you want and that you know what the command is going to do.

Simple DOS commands, execute from the DOS command prompt. Remember DOS is not case sensitive.

- Dir or dir — This will give you the contents of the current directory
- Help — all the commands that are available
- Help dir — gives you all the options available with dir
- cd {dir name}– change directory, you would add the directory name
- cd ../ — moves up the directory tree one level
- cls —clear the DOS window screen
- mkdir {name} -create a directory in current directory
- del {name} -delete the named file
- up arrow key -↑ displays last dos command, you may need to execute doskey to enable
- doskey -enable the repeat command function used by up arrow key

Debian-Linux Shell Scripts

A few hints for making your scripts executable. Not your Python scripts, Python handles that. You can write your script using any text editor, vi or vim, Geany, nano, etc.

- The file name doesn't need an extension.
- Comments are a line starting with a pound sign '#'
- You need to have permission to execute or run the script. After you have saved your script open a terminal window and go to the directory where you saved the script. Type 'ls -l filename' for example. (small letter 'L') The permissions will be shown. Something similar to the following table, third row.

position 1	2	3	4	5	6	7	8	9	10
directory flag	User read	User write	User execute	Group read	Group write	Group execute	Other read	Other write	Other execute
-	r	w	-	r	-	-	r	-	-
-	r	w	x	r	-	-	r	-	-

From a terminal window you can make the script executable if needed. Be in the directory with your script and type chmod u+x filename. Then retype the ls -l filename and you should see the change as shown on row 4 of the preceding table. (NOTE a small letter L) To run the script from the terminal window, be in the same directory and type. ./filename or type . filename (Notice the . and space).

Debian-Linux Commands

Before using understand that many of the commands have options that are not shown here. For those who may have forgotten some simple Linux commands, a very quick refresher course follows. This is only the tip of the iceberg, just listing a few. Before we go any further, a few quick words on commands. They can do damage, they are not very user friendly; they will destroy without asking twice. So make sure the command you enter is the command that you want and that you know what the command is going to do. Remember when you execute a command that involves a filename you may want to proceed the filename with a "./". Example "cat ./filename".

cat filename	list contents of file
cat filename > filename2	copy filename to filename2
cat /etc/debian_version	this will show what version of Debian you are running
cat /etc/os-release	will show misc. os information
cd	change to home directory
cd /	change to root directory
cd ..	move up one level in the directory tree
chgrp newgroup filename	change the group name for the named file
chown newower filename	change the owner of filename to the newowner name
chmod u+x filename	example of changing permission of stk500work for the user to execute
clear	clear the screen can also use Ctrl L
cp filename filename2	copy filename to filname2
date	show current day, date and time
df -h	File systems mounted, size, used, avail Use%, where mounted
dmesg	This will show the devices attached, very useful for finding PL2303 and other serial devices attached
echo $SHELL	to see what shell you are running
echo $PATH	shows current search path
find -name filename	find the specified filename
free -m	display memory used and free
hostname -I	show system current host name
id	what user you are and what groups you are in
ifconfig	display connections information, (eth0, lo, wlan0, etc)
ifconfig -a	show all connections information, mac address next to HWaddr
ip addr show	show connection addresses
kill number	If you need to stop a runaway process, number is the process ID (PID)
lp filename	print filename to default printer
lpstat -t	show default printer
ls	displays current directory
ls -l	displays current directory with permissions (note small Ls)
lsusb	list usb devices running on computer
lsusb -v	run as sudo for a complete list, with v is a verbose list

mkdir filename	make a new directory
more filename	list the file, will do in pages
mv filename filname2	move or rename filename to filname2
pwd	to see what your current directory is
ps –help all	Help information for process's (NOTE there are two '-'
ps -p$$	displays what shell you are running
ps -T or ps	show all processes on this terminal
ps -A	show all processes running on computer
ps aux	show all process running on computer, user, PID & more
pstree	show all processes in a tree format
ps -p$$	show current PID TTY TIME CMD
uname -a	display version and kernel
rm filename	delete file specified
reboot	do an immediate shutdown and then reboot
reset	use when console has character map a mess, resets to standard
rmdir directory	remove specified directory
rm -r directory	remove specified directory and contents of the directory
shutdown -h now	shutdown the computer now, you may need sudo in front of command
who	list all users
whoami	to see what user you are

Under Debian Wheezy 7.6, maybe other versions as well to skip starting the desktop and go straight to a command prompt do the following. 'Ctrl Alt F1' at the Login Screen. If you need to start the desktop, type 'startx', this takes me into Gnome. Which I am having problems with the display, so I don't use it. Really just a note in case you need it.

Advanced Canvas program for Fun

The program is pretty well self descriptive. Several things do need to be pointed out. When you save the file it appears that only what is visible on the Canvas is saved, if you have scrolled away your file may not get the entire image. Second, to use the 'Delete Selected' feature, put anything on the Canvas, then 'Right Click' near the item, then press the 'Delete Selected' button.

```
#Python 3.3.4 Ttk Canvas                          Tk19CanvasADVANCED.py
#RyMax, Inc.  for personal use only  8/8/2014
from tkinter import *
from tkinter.ttk import *
import tkinter.messagebox, tkinter.simpledialog, tkinter.filedialog
import tkinter.colorchooser, tkinter.font
class setup:
        def __init__(self):# define startup colors, brush,etc, setup canvas, toolbars
                self.canvasBackground='tan'
                self.brushColor='black'          # start brush color
```

```python
self.paintTool='line'    # start Tool  'line'=1, 'oval'=2
self.lineWidth=2                # line width
self.linePattern='dash'# line pattern  'solid' = 1, 'dash' =2
self.lineDash=(5)              # pattern for dash only odd segments drawn
self.lineLength=120            # line length
self.lineAngle='H'             # line Angle(1=| Vertical,2 =- Horizontal,3 =\,4=/)
self.ovalWidth=2               # oval width size (x) what to adjust brush size by
self.ovalHeight=3              # oval height size (y) what to adjust brush size by
self.ovalFill='gray'      # for oval default color for fill
self.newFile=''                # setup for insert of new GIF file
self.Canvas = Canvas( root, width =475, height=400,
        borderwidth=5,relief=RAISED, scrollregion=(0,0,1200,800))
self.Canvas.grid(column=0, row=0)
self.Canvas.configure(bg=self.canvasBackground)
self.Canvas.configure(cursor="crosshair")
self.scrollY =Scrollbar(root, orient=VERTICAL, command=self.Canvas.yview)
self.scrollY.grid(row=0, column=1, sticky=NS)
self.scrollX =Scrollbar(root, orient=HORIZONTAL, command=self.Canvas.xview)
self.scrollX.grid(row=1, column=0, sticky=EW)
self.Canvas["yscrollcommand"] = self.scrollY.set
self.Canvas["xscrollcommand"] = self.scrollX.set
self.Canvas.bind( "<B1-Motion>", self.paint )
Label( root, text = "Left Click, Drag mouse to draw" ).grid(column=0,row=3)
self.Canvas.bind("<Button-3>", self.pickItem)            #click right mouse key
root.bind("<Up>", self.moveItemUp)                       #up arrow key
root.bind("<Down>", self.moveItemDown)                   #down arrow key
root.bind("<Left>", self.moveItemLeft)                   #left arrow key
root.bind("<Right>", self.moveItemRight)         #right arrow key
self.myImage=PhotoImage(file='c:/python33/lib/idlelib/icons/python.gif')
self.toolbar = Frame(root)                               # create toolbar Frame
self.toolbar.grid(column=2,row=0,sticky = (N,W,E,S))
self.toolbar2 = Frame(root)                              # second toolbar Frame
self.toolbar2.grid(column=0,row=4,columnspan=3,sticky = (N,W,E,S))
self.BT=Style(self.toolbar)
self.BT.theme_use('classic')
self.BT.configure('TButton')
self.BT.map('TButton',
        foreground=[('disabled','yellow'),('pressed','red'),('active','blue')],
        background=[('disabled','magenta'),('pressed','cyan'),('active','green')],
        highlightcolor=[('focus','green'),('!focus','red')],
        relief=[('pressed', 'groove'),('!pressed', 'ridge')])
self.B1=Button(self.toolbar,text='Select Brush Color',width=15,
        command=self.chBrushColor,style='TButton')
self.B1.grid(column=0,row=0)
self.brushColorLabel=Label(self.toolbar,background=self.brushColor,width =10)
self.brushColorLabel.grid(column=1,row=0)
self.B2=Button(self.toolbar,width=15,command=self.chPaintTool,style='TButton')
self.B2.configure(text="Brush= "+ self.paintTool)
self.B2.grid(column=0,row=1,sticky = NE)
```

```python
        self.B3=Button(self.toolbar, width=15,command=self.chLineWidth,style='TButton')
        self.B3.configure(text="Line Width="+str(self.lineWidth))
        self.B3.grid(column=0,row=2,sticky = NE)
        self.B4=Button(self.toolbar,text="Line Pattern",width=15,
                command=self.Pattern,style='TButton')
        self.B4.configure(text="Line Pattern=" +self.linePattern)
        self.B4.grid(column=0,row=3, sticky = NW)
        self.B5=Button(self.toolbar,width=15,command=self.chLineLength,style='TButton')
        self.B5.configure(text="Line Length= "+str(self.lineLength))
        self.B5.grid(column=0,row=4, sticky = NW)
        self.B6=Button(self.toolbar,width=15,command=self.chLineAngle,style='TButton')
        self.B6.configure(text="Line Angle= "+self.lineAngle)
        self.B6.grid(column=0,row=5, sticky = NW)
        self.B7=Button(self.toolbar,width=15,command=self.chOvalHeight,style='TButton')
        self.B7.configure( text="Oval Height= "+str(self.ovalHeight))
        self.B7.grid(column=0,row=6, sticky = NW)
        self.B8=Button(self.toolbar,width=15,command=self.chOvalWidth,style='TButton')
        self.B8.configure( text="Oval Width= "+str(self.ovalWidth))
        self.B8.grid(column=0,row=7, sticky = NW)
        self.B9=Button(self.toolbar,width=15,command=self.chOvalFill,style='TButton',
                text="Oval Fill Color").grid(column=0,row=8, sticky = NW)
        self.ovalFillLabel = Label(self.toolbar,background = self.ovalFill, width =10)
        self.ovalFillLabel.grid(column=1,row=8)
        self.B10=Button(self.toolbar,width=15,command=self.chDash,style='TButton')
        self.B10.configure( text="Line Dash Size= "+str(self.lineDash))
        self.B10.grid(column=0,row=9, sticky = NW)
#       second Toolbar items
        self.B11=Button(self.toolbar2,width=15,command=self.openFile,style='TButton',
                text="Open File").grid(column=0,row=0, sticky = NW)
        self.B12=Button(self.toolbar2,width=15,command=self.saveFile,style='TButton',
                text="Save File").grid(column=1,row=0, sticky = NW)
        self.B13=Button(self.toolbar2,width=15,command=self.cleanCanvas,style='TButton',
                text="Clear Canvas File").grid(column=2,row=0, sticky = NW)
        self.B14=Button(self.toolbar2,width=15,command=self.drawSomeStuff,
                style='TButton',text="Draw Canned Stuff").grid(column=3,row=0,sticky=NW)
        self.B15=Button(self.toolbar2,width=15,command=self.deleteItem,style='TButton',
                text="Delete Selected").grid(column=4,row=0, sticky = NW)
    def paint( self, event ):
        x1, y1 =(event.x, event.y)      # mouse x and y values
        if self.paintTool == 'line':
            if self.lineAngle=='V':         # vertical line
                x2 ,y2 = (x1, y1+self.lineLength)
            if self.lineAngle=='H':#horizontal line
                x2 ,y2 = (x1+self.lineLength, y1)
            if self.lineAngle=='\\':#line at 45% \
                x2 ,y2 = (x1+self.lineLength, y1+35)        #add 35 to get angle
            if self.lineAngle=='/':#line at -45% /
                x2 ,y2 = (x1+self.lineLength, y1-35)#subtract 35 to get angle
            if self.linePattern == 'dash':
```

```python
                    self.Canvas.create_line(x1, y1 ,x2, y2, fill = self.brushColor,
                        width=self.lineWidth, dash=self.lineDash)  # creates sticks

                else:
                    self.Canvas.create_line(x1, y1 ,x2, y2, fill = self.brushColor,
                        width=self.lineWidth)  # creates sticks
        if self.paintTool == 'oval':
                x2, y2 = (x1+self.ovalWidth, y1+self.ovalHeight)
                self.Canvas.create_oval(x1,y1,x2,y2,
                        outline=self.brushColor, fill=self.ovalFill, tags='ellip')
    def chBrushColor(self):
        temp=tkinter.colorchooser.askcolor(initialcolor=self.brushColor)
        if temp==(None, None):
                return
        self.brushColor=temp[1]
        self.brushColorLabel.configure(background =self.brushColor)
    def chPaintTool(self):
        temp=self.paintTool
        temp2 = tkinter.simpledialog.askinteger("Paint Tool",
        "Enter Integer\n"+"line=1\n"+ "Oval=2\n"+"Current Tool= "+
                self.paintTool,minvalue=1, maxvalue=2)
        if temp2 ==None:
                self.paintTool=temp
                return
        if temp2 == 1:
                self.paintTool='line'
        else:
                self.paintTool='oval'
        self.B2.configure(text="Brush= "+ self.paintTool)
    def chLineWidth(self):
        temp = self.lineWidth
        self.lineWidth=tkinter.simpledialog.askinteger("Line Width","Enter Integer\n"+
                "Current Size= "+str(self.lineWidth),minvalue=1, maxvalue=40)
        if self.lineWidth==None:
                self.lineWidth=temp
        self.B3.configure(text="Line Width="+str(self.lineWidth))
    def Pattern(self):
        temp = self.linePattern
        temp2=tkinter.simpledialog.askinteger("Line Pattern",
                "Enter Integer\n"+
                " solid line =1\n"+
                " dash line  =2\n"+
                "Current Line Pattern= "+self.linePattern,minvalue=1, maxvalue=2)
        if temp2 == None:
                return
        elif temp2==1:
                self.linePattern='solid'
        else:
                self.linePattern='dash'
```

```python
            self.B4.configure(text="Line Pattern="+ self.linePattern)
    def chLineLength(self):
        temp = self.lineLength
        self.lineLength=tkinter.simpledialog.askinteger("Line Length","Enter Integer\n"
                +"Current Width="+str(self.lineLength),minvalue=1,maxvalue=240)
        if self.lineLength == None:
            self.lineLength = temp
        self.B5.configure(text="Line Length= "+str(self.lineLength))
    def chLineAngle(self):
        temp = self.lineAngle
        temp2=tkinter.simpledialog.askinteger("Line Angle",
                "Enter Integer\n"+"1 for V vertical\n"+"2 for H horizontal\n"+
                "3 for / 45 right\n"+"4 for \ 45 left\n"+
                "Current Line Angle= "+str(self.lineAngle),minvalue=1, maxvalue=4)
        if self.lineAngle == None:
            self.lineAngle = temp
        if temp2 == 1:
            self.lineAngle='V'
        if temp2 == 2:
            self.lineAngle='H'
        if temp2 == 3:
            self.lineAngle='\\'
        if temp2 == 4:
            self.lineAngle='/'
        self.B6.configure(text="Line Angle= "+self.lineAngle)
    def chOvalHeight(self):
        temp=self.ovalHeight
        self.ovalHeight = tkinter.simpledialog.askinteger("Oval Height Size",
        "Enter Integer\n"+"Current Size= "+str(self.ovalHeight),minvalue=1,maxvalue=300)
        if self.ovalHeight ==None:
            self.ovalHeight=temp
        self.B7.configure( text="Oval Height= "+str(self.ovalHeight))
    def chOvalWidth(self):
        temp=self.ovalWidth
        self.ovalWidth = tkinter.simpledialog.askinteger("Oval Width Size",
        "Enter Integer\n"+"Current Size= "+str(self.ovalWidth),minvalue=1,maxvalue=300)
        if self.ovalWidth ==None:
            self.ovalWidth=temp
        self.B8.configure(text="Oval Width= "+str(self.ovalWidth))
    def chOvalFill(self):
        temp=self.ovalFill
        resp = tkinter.messagebox.askyesno('Transparent?','Transparent oval, click yes')
        if resp == True:
            self.ovalFill="          #set to null for transparent
        if resp == False:
            try:
                temp=tkinter.colorchooser.askcolor(initialcolor=self.ovalFill)
            except:  # will get exeption if was previously transparent
                temp=tkinter.colorchooser.askcolor(initialcolor='black')
```

```python
                if temp==(None, None):
                    return
                self.ovalFill=temp[1]
            self.ovalFillLabel.configure(background =self.ovalFill)
        def chDash(self):
            temp = self.lineDash
            self.lineDash=tkinter.simpledialog.askinteger("Line Dash Size","Enter Integer\n"+
                "Current Size= "+str(self.lineDash),minvalue=1,maxvalue=255)
            if self.lineDash==None:
                self.lineDash=temp
            self.B10.configure(text="Line Dash Size= "+str(self.lineDash))
#Buttons toolbar2 items
    def openFile(self):
        self.newFile=tkinter.filedialog.askopenfilename(title='Open GIF File',
            filetypes=(('GIF files','*.gif'),('PPM files','*.ppm')))
        self.newFile = PhotoImage(file=self.newFile)
        self.Canvas.create_image(275,275,image=self.newFile)
    def saveFile(self):
        if tkinter.messagebox.askyesno("Create", "Create new file?"):
            fp=tkinter.simpledialog.askstring("Name for Postscript File",
                "Enter file name \n(.ps) file extension automatically added")
            self.Canvas.postscript(file=fp+".ps", colormode = 'color')
    def cleanCanvas(self):
        self.Canvas.delete(ALL)
    def drawSomeStuff(self):#    start       end              Draw some standard stuff
        self.Canvas.create_line(125, 150, 175, 150, width=1,tags='line1')#horizontal
        self.Canvas.create_line(225, 150, 275, 150, width=2,tags='line2')#horizontal
        self.Canvas.create_line(200, 85, 200, 135,  width=5,tags='line3')#vertical
        self.Canvas.create_line(200, 165, 200, 215, width=9,tags='line4')#vertical
        self.Canvas.create_oval(125,150,200,250, width=5, fill='blue',
            outline='red', activefill='green')#ellipse fits inside a rectangle,
                #top left(125,150) and bottom right(200,250) points are defined
        p1= (300,200)          #bottom common point for a Tetrahedron
        p2= (250,100)          #top left front
        p3= (280,110)          #top right front
        #back to common for point
        p4=(290,90)            #triangle to right side
        self.Canvas.create_polygon(p1,p2,p3,p1,p4,p3,p2,p4,fill=",width=1,
            splinesteps=1,outline='black')
        self.Canvas.create_image(20,20,image=self.myImage)
        self.Canvas.create_text(50,50, activefill='red',text="My text for now")
    def deleteItem(self):
        try: self.Canvas.delete(self.currentItem)
        except:pass           #probably none selected
    def pickItem(self, event):#for mouse
        self.currentItem = self.Canvas.find_closest(event.x, event.y)
        try: self.itemTags=self.Canvas.gettags(self.currentItem)
        except: pass
    def moveItemUp(self,event):
```

```
                print ('move it up')
                for i in range(0, 5):                              #number of times to move
                        self.Canvas.move(self.currentItem, 0, -3)#how much to move each time
                self.Canvas.update()
        def moveItemDown(self,event):
                for i in range(0, 5):
                        self.Canvas.move(self.currentItem, 0, 3)
                self.Canvas.update()
        def moveItemLeft(self,event):
                for i in range (0, 5):
                        self.Canvas.move(self.currentItem, -3, 0)
                self.Canvas.update()
        def moveItemRight(self,event):
                for i in range (0, 5):
                        self.Canvas.move(self.currentItem, 3, 0)
                self.Canvas.update()
if __name__=='__main__':
        root = Tk()
        root.title( "RyMax Window on the world" )
        root.geometry( "700x500+50+30" ) #width, height, placement y  x
        setup()
        mainloop()
```

Reference Sites

Python

www.sourceforge.net

www.learnpython.org

www.tutorialspoint.com/python/index.htm

https://developers.google.com/edu/python

http://anh.cs.luc.edu/python/hands-on/handsonHtml/handson.html

Tkinter/Ttk

http://www.tkdocs.com/tutorial/windows.html

https://www.tcl.tk/man/tcl/TkCmd/colors.htm

http://wiki.tcl.tk/37973   Source for Ttk Widget Color configure

http://infohost.nmt.edu/tcc/help/pubs/tkinter/web/index.html

http://pages.cpsc.ucalgary.ca/~saul/personal/archives/Tcl-Tk_stuff/tcl_examples/

http://effbot.org/tkinterbook/

http://www.tutorialspoint.com/python/python_gui_programming.htm

http://www.beedub.com/book/2nd/TKINTRO.doc.html

http://zetcode.com/gui/tkinter/menustoolbars/

http://infohost.nmt.edu/tcc/help/pubs/tkinter/web/menu.html

http://www.tutorialspoint.com/python/tk_messagebox.htm

http://www.tutorialspoint.com/python/tk_canvas.htm

http://users.tricity.wsu.edu/~bobl/cpts481/tkinter_nmt.pdf

Sqlite3

https://docs.python.org/3.4/library/sqlite3.html

http://www.sqlite.org/datatype3.html

http://zetcode.com/db/sqlitepythontutorial/

http://www.lemonsoftware.eu/goodies/python:sqlitepy

Linux

http://steve-parker.org/sh/intro.shtml
http://linuxtutorial.info/modules.php?name=MContent&pageid=329
http://en.wikibooks.org/wiki/Linux_For_Newbies/Command_Line

www.ingramcontent.com/pod-product-compliance
Lightning Source LLC
Chambersburg PA
CBHW060449060326

40689CB00020B/4477